Contents

It's our welfare

report of the **citizens' commission ON THE FUTURE OF THE welfare state**

Peter Beresford and Michael Turner

It's **our** welfare: report of the Citizens' Commision on the Future of the
Welfare State

Published 1997
on behalf of the Citizens' Commission on the Future of the Welfare State
by the National Institute for Social Work
5 Tavistock Place, London WC1H 9SN

Citizens' Commission on the Future of the Welfare State
Tempo House, 15 Falcon Road, London SW11 2PJ

The Commission was supported by the Baring Foundation and
Community Care magazine.

ISBN 1 899942 17 3

A catalogue record for this book is available from the British Library.

Design by Pat Kahn
Illustrations on pages xiii–xv by Simon Kewer, and on pages160–2 by
People First

Printed by Meridian Print Centre Ltd,
Perkins Industrial Estate, Mansfield Road, Derby DE21 4AW
Telephone: 01332 200 600

Acknowledgements

The Citizens' Commission has many thanks to offer. First we must thank all the individuals and groups who took the trouble to contribute evidence. We know how much effort people put into doing this, generally with very limited material resources and we want to offer our sincere thanks. We also want to thank those organisations and individuals who put us in touch with local and national groups of welfare state service users and the many people who helped put together the meetings which we held. Thanks must also go to the Baring Foundation which had faith in this project, and without whose support welfare state service users would continue to have no voice in the debate about the future of welfare.

We would like to thank *Community Care* magazine and its editor Terry Philpot for financial and practical support. Our thanks also go to the National Institute for Social Work, particularly Margaret Hogan, Audrey McLeod, Pearl Sebastian and Daphne Statham and to Tessa Harding, now of Help The Aged. Our thanks also go to Pat Kahn for the help she gave the Commission as graphic designer. Finally thanks to Suzy Croft whose unpaid work as the Commission's administrator helped both to ensure its smooth operation and that good communication was always maintained.

Recommendations

Commitment to welfare

- The state funding of the welfare state must be given much higher political priority.
- The cost of services, like long term care, should be shared through taxation and older people not expected to meet the bill themselves.
- Needs identified in social care assessments must be met.

Supporting independence

- The welfare state in future must be based on the principle of supporting people to live independently rather than keeping them in dependence. Welfare state benefits and services policy should be integrated and both informed by this principle.
- The shift to 'targetting' in welfare state services should be halted and policy and provision seek to meet need regardless of 'race', gender, class, age, disability, religion or sexual identity.
- Government policy should shift from subsidising low pay through the benefits system, to a programme of major investment in state economic and employment policy, to generate good quality, skilled employment, if people are to escape the poverty and welfare traps.
- Full and effective anti-discrimination legislation for disabled people should be introduced, based on a social model of disability.

Education and training for inclusion

- Education must prioritise the inclusion of all children and young people in mainstream schools and enable them to develop their skills and abilities to their full potential.

- There must be large scale government investment in employment training for young people and adults which equips people with recognised skills and is linked with and leads to good quality jobs.

Flexible, sensitive services

- Increased flexibility should be built into the benefits system so that people are not prevented from benefiting from educational, training and employment opportunities.
- Increased flexibility is essential in support services to ensure that they respond rapidly and appropriately to people's changing needs and can be started and stopped as required.

Combatting poverty

- State benefit and pension levels must be raised to relate them to the real costs of daily living and to safeguard people from the destructive effects of poverty.
- The exclusion of 16–18 year olds from receipt of benefits must be ended.
- A minimum wage should be introduced set at a level which will keep people out of the poverty and benefit traps.

Accessing services and support

- Accurate and accessible information should be provided to ensure that welfare state service users are aware of what services and support are available and to what they are entitled.
- Independent advocacy should be made widely availabe with financial support from central government.

Respecting welfare state service users

- A major retraining programme is required for welfare state workers, particularly in the benefits system, as part of a new commitment to ensure that service users are treated positively, sympathetically and with respect, without stigma or hostility.
- Guidelines and a code of conduct must be developed in full

consultation with welfare state service users' organisations to control media and political attacks on them.

Involving users

- All future plans for welfare state reform should include a programme of effective and broad-based consultation with service users.

- There needs to be a new emphasis on quality in welfare state services with service users fully involved in standard setting, monitoring and evaluation.

- Legislative requirements for effective user involvement in welfare policy and practice should be extended to both the benefits system and all welfare state services.

- Full and effective freedom of information legislation should be introduced guaranteeing full access to and involvement in all information held on people.

- Effective arrangements for complaint and redress in all welfare state services should be introduced after widespread consultation.

- Service user trainers should be fully involved in all professional training for welfare state benefits and services.

- Organisations controlled by service users should receive a much larger proportion of public spending to voluntary and non-statutory organisations, to support the development of user-controlled services and user-led alternatives.

Summary

The aim of the Citizens' Commission was to enable welfare state service users, for the first time, to have their say in the discussion about the future of the welfare state. These are some of its main findings.

The consistency of the findings
Welfare state service users have an important perspective to contribute to welfare state discussions which they are willing and able to offer. There was great consistency in what they said and in their concerns and hopes.

Enquiry between equals
The fact that the Commission's inquiry was based on welfare state service users giving evidence on equal terms to people with shared experience and understanding, made possible a fuller and franker understanding of welfare from the perspective of service users. The value and importance of this cannot be overestimated at a time when welfare state service users are constantly under attack and debate about welfare is defensive, heavily politicised and ideologically loaded.

Independence not dependence
A central concern of welfare state service users was to be independent. While they wanted to be active members of society, they frequently felt trapped in welfare. They made clear the importance they attached to getting paid work. They saw employment as a right rather than an obligation and emphasised the need for the creation of good quality employment, rather than work at any price, to bring people out of the welfare system and out of poverty.

Support for independence

Improving the availability and quality of social care support will enable its users to live independently and family and friends who are increasingly required to support them to share the same rights and opportunities in society as other people. Lone parents and two-parent families made the same argument for affordable and low cost child care.

Paying for welfare

More political priority should be given to welfare and it should be paid for by taxation. Welfare state service users believed that the costs of welfare can and should be met by them being shared. For example, older people should not be expected to meet the cost of long term care. Welfare state service users contribute to the cost of welfare through taxation like everyone else. Placing more emphasis on creating good quality employment will reduce the welfare bill and help pay for it.

The importance of benefits *and* services

Welfare state service users had much to say about welfare services as well as benefits. The two are equally important and need to be considered in conjunction with each other, although discussion so far has mainly only focused on benefits.

The negative experience of welfare

Service users' experience and views of the current welfare state were generally very negative. This applied across benefits and services, including health, education and social services. While there were exceptions, they reported practice and provision which was of poor quality, inadequate and stigmatic. Benefit levels were singled out for particular attention as being grossly inadequate for people to live on.

Excluded as second class citizens

People also expressed strong feelings of being disenfranchised and disempowered. People's exclusion from the welfare state debate was just one expression of this. They felt they had little or no control politically, socially, economically and often personally over their lives. The problem of social exclusion emerges as much more than that conceived narrowly in terms of people not being integrated into society through paid employment.

The reality of welfare

While the welfare reforms of recent years were supposed to resolve problems associated with traditional provision, from service users' perspective, there are few if any signs of problems under the old system being resolved, but rather of new problems being created. They reported inadequate, unresponsive and frequently unreliable treatment from both the benefits and the service systems.

The importance of education and training

Welfare state service users saw education and training as the route out of welfare into decent employment. Both policies have so far failed to ensure children and adults the qualifications and opportunities to which they should be entitled. Welfare state service users were particularly concerned about training and educational opportunities of children and young people, since they represent their future and that of society overall.

Inadequate information

Welfare state service users identified lack of information as one of the key obstacles in the way of gaining the support which they needed. People were denied access to support and services to which they were entitled for want of accessible, reliable and independent information. This applied to both welfare benefits and welfare services. This caused great hardship and made many of their difficulties worse. Members of minority ethnic groups identified the lack of appropriate and accessible information as one of the contributing factors which denied them full and equal access to the welfare state.

More say in welfare

One of the main problems which welfare state service users identified was that it was frequently insensitive, unresponsive and unaccountable to them. They felt they generally had little say or control over it and how it treated them. As a result they were often treated carelessly and badly. The worst treatment participants reported was by the benefits system. Existing provisions for redress in both welfare benefits and service systems were inadequate.

Increasing the say of service users was seen as an important way of ensuring that future welfare state services were of good quality, flexible, appropriate and accountable.

Wasting resources

Service users stressed the need for welfare state funding to be used more effectively and efficiently. Welfare reforms since the 1980s had placed much emphasis on 'value for money', reductions in waste, bureaucracy and unnecessary public expenditure. In their evidence service users said that these reforms were themselves a frequent and major cause of waste and inefficiency.

Welfare users under attack

While people receiving welfare services frequently reported the negative treatment they received at their hands, this seemed to be linked to much broader social and public attitudes and values. Continuing political and media attacks on welfare state service users were having direct and destructive effects on them. This made some people reluctant to seek support however desperate their circumstances. Attacks on welfare and on its users have been closely linked. Years of blaming welfare state service users has made them the subject of a climate of fear and division. A climate of fear and hostility has been generated around both. There needs to be change in public and political attitudes towards people who use welfare.

Illustrated summary

This summary of the Citizens' Commission Report is provided for non-readers and people who have difficulty with reading.

These are the main things that people who use welfare state services told us:

They value being talked to by people like them

They want to be independent

Many feel trapped in welfare

They want decent paid jobs

Welfare can and should be paid for by everyone in their taxes

There should be more good jobs, then it would be easier to pay for welfare

Benefits and services are *both* important

They have more bad than good experiences of welfare

People who use welfare feel they often aren't allowed to be full members of society

Education and training are important for people to be independent. So is personal assistance and child care

People want more information about welfare

They want to have more say in welfare in future

Politicians and the media should stop attacking people who use welfare

Introduction

There has never been so much uncertainty about the future of the welfare state. Politicians say it must change. Welfare state service users have come under increasing media attack as 'dependent' and a costly drain on taxpayers. Yet they have had virtually no say in the discussion that is now taking place about welfare's future. They have been allowed no chance to answer their critics or offer their own proposals for the future. Yet their first hand experience means they have an important perspective to offer.

This book offers the first Report of what people who use welfare state services want for the future of welfare, based on an inquiry undertaken by welfare state service users themselves. In doing this it breaks new ground. But it is also a modest project. We make no claims to speak for millions of people. Like most welfare state service users, our resources were strictly limited. But what we do know is that as welfare state service users ourselves, we have spoken to and heard from *more* users of welfare state services about the future of the welfare state than either politicians, academics or other 'experts'.

We are not saying that we are offering the 'last word' on what kind of future service users want for the welfare state. Instead we hope that this Report will be seen as an important opening to a much broader debate and encourage more efforts to speak on equal terms to many more current and potential users of welfare to establish their views and ideas. How else will welfare in future avoid the errors which have been made in the past?

The discussion about welfare, however, has so far been paternalistic, conducted over most people's heads and largely without them taking part. This is why we decided to take our own initiative and why it takes the form it does. The debate about welfare has generally been framed as a choice between the old state paternalism and the new private sector self-help. But we also want to draw a different distinction.

Current political changes and broader dissatisfaction with social policy have led to *two* new challenges to traditional welfare policy and thinking. The first challenge has been the pressure for a return to market and private sector methods of meeting needs which we have just mentioned. This can be summed up as a switch to 'looking after ourselves', through private pensions, insurance, health care and other services, like day nurseries and nursery education and long term care. It has been linked with a strong sense that the state has failed. The second challenge has been the demand for people's much greater involvement in shaping their own welfare, in terms of having more say and control over policies, agencies and services which affect them and which impact on their lives, *whoever* supplies them.

The rhetoric associated with these two developments has been remarkably similar, emphasising people's choice, say, opportunity and 'empowerment'. Yet they are generally very different to each other and often in conflict. Critics of the first argue that the new enthusiasm for the market is backward-looking and that it has been the market's longstanding failure to meet needs which first led to the search for state alternatives. Critics of the second argue that it is unrealistic and impossible; that it is neither feasible nor desirable to involve everyone in the process of policy and provision; that many people would not want to be involved and that it would be impossibly costly as everyone pressed for everything they wanted.

The weight of evidence highlighting the limitations of market-led welfare is growing. But what evidence there is about more 'user-led' initiatives from the growing experience which now exists, points in the opposite direction, indicating better, more cost-effective, accountable and flexible policy and provision.

This Report and the Commission inquiry upon which it is based, are part of this emerging tradition. They reflect a much broader development: where the goal is not to offer a particular prescription or blueprint, but to enable people to develop their own. The aim of this book is to access the voice of people who are not powerful politically, economically or socially; many of whom don't have the base of political parties, trade unions or business to back them up. These were the people the welfare state was set up to serve and who its critics say it has failed. It is time to hear what they have to say.

Structure of the Report

To help readers check the results of the Commission's inquiry quickly, the book begin with three short sections. These are first, the recommendations of the Commission; second, a summary of our findings; and finally, an illustrated summary, designed to be more accessible for non-readers and for people who have difficulty with reading. The Commission made a commitment to *People First*, the organisation of people with learning difficulties, to provide such a summary.

The body of the book is organised in four parts. Part One sets out the background to the Report. Readers may want to go straight past this and look first at Part Two. This brings together the views, experience and proposals of welfare state service users who took part in the Commission. It is the largest and most important part of the Report.

Part One sets the scene for readers who are interested. Chapter One explains the background to the Commission and why we thought it was important to enable people who use welfare state services to have a say in the debate that is taking place about the future of welfare. In Chapter Two we describe how we set up the Commission. Chapter Three explains how we carried out the Commission's work. We have set this out in some detail so that other groups and organisations which might want to do something similar can see how we did it.

Part Two sets out what service users say about welfare. This includes their views about existing provision as well as their proposals for the future. Chapter Four focuses on their evidence about the welfare state generally and about the benefits system. Chapter Five examines their views about other welfare state services, including health, education and community care. Chapter Six looks at a number of more general themes which participants identified which have important implications for the future of welfare.

In Part Three, we analyse and draw together what welfare state service users said to provide the Report's findings and conclusions. Chapter Seven analyses and collates the evidence which we received. Chapter Eight summarises the findings and conclusions emerging from the Commission's enquiry.

The final section of the book, Part Four, includes references and a series of Appendices. The latter detail members of the

Commission and the evidence which we received. They also include additional information to enable readers to find out more about how we actually undertook the work of the Commission. We hope other people will be able to build on our experience. It is not intended as a blueprint, but to offer support and assistance.

PART 1

The Citizens' Commission

Background to the Commission

The centrality of welfare

There are few more important public policies than welfare. In the UK, the welfare state costs an estimated £90 billion a year, with social security spending making up one third of all government expenditure. In recent times, welfare policy has played a crucial part in general elections in the UK, US and other countries. Whatever we think of it, welfare policy affects all our lives. We all contribute to and receive its services in one way or another. Many of us may also work for it. It is a major employer. It is the biggest service industry in the UK. The National Health Service alone is the biggest organisation in Europe. Yet welfare tends to be treated as a poor relation. It usually only makes the headlines when something goes wrong and there is something or someone to attack or condemn. Otherwise it scores low on news value. At best it is seen as 'worthy but dull' and relegated to the back pages. The welfare state service user who makes a false benefits claim or who it is thought could get a job, but doesn't, is news. The welfare state service user who desperately wants to get a job but can't, or who has ideas to offer to improve the system, isn't.

Political agreement that the welfare state must change

While many politicians may find welfare boring, this has not stopped it being the focus for some of their biggest arguments and differences. Few issues are more politically contentious than welfare. The political right and left have had their own very different and opposed views about it, although recent realignments have begun to change this. There is no agreement about what shape the welfare state should take. But there is one point over which there is consensus. This is that the welfare state must change. Politicians and experts across the board are agreed about this. There have already been major changes in countries as diverse as the US, Australia, Sweden, Germany and the UK and there is a strong sense that there is much more to come. While different countries may be at different stages in a process of change, there seems to be little doubt that all are headed in the same general direction towards fundamental change in welfare. Current political and expert debate over the welfare state is prompted by concerns about its cost, its creation of 'passivity' and 'dependence', demographic changes which will mean a large increase in the number of very old people in the population in the twenty first century, the 'globalisation' of economics and the failure of the welfare state to achieve its aims and meet individual needs.

The narrowness of debate about welfare

There is now a major debate about the future of the welfare state. Government, political parties, academics and professionals have all played a part in developing it. But so far there has been little public discussion about the future of the welfare state and debates have been dominated by politicians and conventional experts.

Neither political parties nor experts have made possible a real public discussion on welfare. The debate has been dominated by the same old voices. Politicians, academics, think tanks with vested ideological interests and organisations run for welfare state service users rather than by them, have so far dominated the discussion. The debate has been characterised by the exclusion of welfare state services users, despite increasing calls from all sides for their involvement in welfare policy and services.

Major enquiries into the welfare state like the Dahrendorf Commission on wealth creation and social cohesion, the Anson Committee report on the future of pensions and the Joseph Rowntree Foundation study of income and wealth have had no place for welfare state service users.

Both Conservative administrations and the Labour Party have embarked on major policy reviews and discussions about the future of welfare, but neither has involved welfare state service users to any major extent. The Conservatives have undertaken no serious consultation with welfare state service users. Yet in the context of their community care reforms, they have repeatedly emphasised the importance of local social services and health authorities consulting service users, introduced legislation and regulations requiring it and stressed that 'needs-led' services are the central aim of their reforms. There has been increasing recognition from all political quarters of the importance of involving service users and of them having a say and choice in policy and practice. But this has not been reflected in debates about welfare.

The Labour Party's Commission on Social Justice is an important example of the problem. (Commission on Social Justice, 1994) The Commission was set up to undertake a radical and independent review of the welfare state. But it quickly came in for criticism for its failure to include welfare recipients alongside the 'great and the good'. Bob Holman, the welfare commentator, wrote:

> I must express my concern that the Commission's membership does not include unemployed people, those on low incomes or residents of the inner cities and council estates. This exclusion reinforces the myth that they are unable to contribute to serious debate and analysis.
> *Holman*, 1993

In an editorial, the *New Statesman* said:

> The Commission is not exactly packed with iconoclasts. Not does it include a single person with direct experience of poverty – an omission that eliminates a valuable source of ideas, and perpetuates the prescriptive paternalism that underpins the foundations of the welfare state.
> *New Statesman and Society*, 1993

There has been a long history of such exclusion in the formulation of the welfare state from Beveridge onwards. A series of landmark committees and inquiries into personal social services and broader social policy failed to include the views of service users, from the Seebohm Report to the Barclay Report, the Younghusband Report to the Griffiths Report. Initiatives to involve service users have been the exception rather than the rule and they have generally been limited and partial. For example, the Support Force which was set up in the wake of the community care reforms only included service users at the last minute and like the Department of Health's National Users and Carers Group established to monitor them, its remit was limited and confined to community care.

Radical changes have already been made in welfare in the UK

without any semblance of public debate or involvement. These changes range from the creation of the Child Support Agency, to the introduction of Incapacity Benefit, Job Seeker's Allowance, workfare and the withdrawal of benefits from asylum seekers.

The debate about the future of welfare has been a narrow one in other ways too. The political right and left have both been constrained by short-termism and their own ideological and political preoccupations. Conservative administrations have been stuck with the need to reduce a multi-million pound deficit and pacify a right wing fiercely opposed to state intervention and public spending. The Labour Party has been preoccupied with its image and desperately trying to cast off its reputation as the party of high taxation and high spending. Both are concerned about the high cost of welfare. The debate has largely been framed in traditional left-right terms of old universalism versus new-style targetting, even though political positions have really moved on and problems with both approaches have long been evident.

Because this narrow debate has been overly shaped by the political and ideological concerns of the main protagonists, it is far from clear whether their objections to and proposals for welfare are based on practical and policy requirements, or follow from their own preoccupations, needs and interests.

The importance of involving people in discussions about welfare

The most important problem with the narrow debate which there has been so far about welfare is that it flies in the face of arguments of both left and right, government and opposition, that it is crucial for citizens to be involved in public policy and services if they are to have choice and opportunity, and if they are to be active partners in, rather than passive recipients of, provision. This is especially important in the context of welfare, because of the central place arguments and ideas about the 'dependence' of welfare state service users have gained in political and media discussions about welfare. So people's involvement in the debate about welfare is consistent with politicians' own rhetoric. There are also a range of other more substantial reasons for including welfare state service users in the discussion. These reasons include:

• to provide full and balanced information and views;

- to make sure that people understand and have a sense of ownership of new developments;
- to reflect the many different needs which welfare must take account of according to age, 'race', gender, disability and sexual identity;

and because:

- if fundamental changes are being made in policy as important as welfare, then the fullest possible discussion is necessary;
- changes in welfare affect all of us and we all have an investment in them;
- all the public policy initiatives, from tower blocks to urban planning, where people have not been asked what they want, have been human disasters and costly failures;
- existing evidence shows that most people want to be involved in decision-making over key policies affecting them;
- making decisions for people is inconsistent with the increasing political emphasis on discouraging 'dependence' and passivity;
- we live in a democracy, which places a premium on citizens' right to a voice in what is done and what happens to them.

Why the Citizens' Commission?

The idea of the Citizens' Commission grew out of a general concern about the failure to include welfare state service users in discussions about the future of welfare and recognition of the need to do this if proposals for reform were to get it right.

What immediately prompted the idea was the failure of the Labour Party's Commission on Social Justice to include welfare state service users in its membership. At the time the Commission on Social Justice was presented as a radical attempt to rethink welfare. If efforts to involve service users in existing inquiries were unsuccessful, then it looked as though service users would have to establish their own inquiry.

One of us wrote to Donald Dewar, the then Labour Party Social Security Spokesperson, in 1992 asking if he and his colleagues would consider including people with experience of poverty alongside academics and policymakers when deciding on the membership of the Commission, saying that 'they are the real experts and can't be criticised for having any axe to grind'. (29 September 1992) Donald Dewar replied that he 'took our point' but that it would be 'very difficult to put together a 'representative' body as there are so many interests that have something to contribute'. (5 October 1992) Thus the Labour Party seemed to have decided that since there were so many poor people who might be included in the Commission, it couldn't include any at all. But as Viv Lindow, one of the service users appointed by the government to its Community Care Support Force, had said earlier: 'Representativeness is a double standard which is usually applied only to service users.'

Precedents for the Commission

There are precedents for such a Commission which show that it can work and which provide helpful experiences to be drawn on. These include the Greater London Council's Claimants' Commission, where people on benefits undertook their own investigation of the benefits system, (Croft and Beresford, 1990) and the European Network of Women's European Tribunal of Women with Experience of Poverty, which brought together delegates from EC countries to share their experience and develop their demands. (Croft, 1989) In 1990, there was a national meeting bringing together people with direct experience of poverty and anti-poverty professionals which highlighted the importance and feasibility of involving poor people in poverty discussions and anti-poverty action. (Lister and Beresford, 1991) In 1996 the participation sub-group of the coordinating committee for the UN International Year for the Eradication of poverty brought together people with experience of poverty from different parts of the country to discuss their ideas and proposals for combating poverty.

The context of the Commission

The aim of this publication is to report what welfare state service users have to say about the welfare state. It may be helpful though to try briefly to put their comments in the context of existing discussion about welfare. We cannot hope to offer a comprehensive account of this and that is not our aim, but it may be helpful to identify some of the key features of conventional debate. (For a helpful guide to the conventional debate about welfare, see Hills, 1993.) We have already touched on some of these.

The focus of debate has reflected the priorities and concerns of policy makers rather than service users and has generally been pitched at a macro rather than micro level. Discussion has been preoccupied with the benefits system, although the welfare state has traditionally been conceived in much broader terms, encompassing a wider range of policies, services and provision. While, for example, 'long term care' has also emerged in recent years as a key policy concern, it has tended to be treated as a separate issue. There are also signs of convergence in both the focus and prescriptions of the different political discussions. Four central concerns can be identified in mainstream discussion about the future of welfare. Central to all of them are ideas and controversies about the role of the state in welfare. They are concerned with how to:

- deal with changed political, social and economic circumstances
- pay for welfare
- prevent welfare perpetuating perceived 'dependence'
- organise welfare to work 'efficiently'.

Specific areas of concern in debates about welfare include:

- demographic change: particularly the large increase predicted in some quarters in the numbers and proportion of very old people in the population and the reduced proportion of people in paid employment;
- a commitment to a plural supply of welfare, including the private and voluntary sectors and 'informal helping networks';
- a strong reluctance to increase public expenditure on welfare;
- a change in emphasis from making collective to individual provision: from taxation to saving for welfare;
- the association of welfare with 'dependency' and a disaffiliated 'underclass';
- public policy for those identified as unable to 'provide for themselves';
- the increase in means-tested benefits;

- the shift from 'universalist' welfare to 'targetted' welfare, and the relation between 'universalism' and 'particularism'.

In this Report, we try to go a step further back, starting with what welfare is for, rather than beginning with its 'hows' and 'whys' as policy and provision. Our aim has been to return to welfare's starting point, that is to say, what citizens themselves might want from welfare as service users. This key level of discussion often seems to have been taken for granted or based upon expert and political assumptions. We thought that it was important to go back to base here.

The aim of the Commission

The idea at the heart of this independent Commission was *involvement*. Its purpose was to provide an opportunity for people most affected by the welfare state – those on the receiving end – to say what kind of welfare state they wanted to see for the future. The central aim of the Commission was to help ensure that recipients of welfare state services could have a voice in its future. It was intended to produce a Report of the Commission's findings as a basis for future discussion and campaigning. Equally important was the way in which we sought to undertake this work. The Commission was based on the belief that the best way of involving welfare state service users was for people with experience as service users to do it *themselves*. As we put it in one of our leaflets:

> The Commission will be made up of welfare state service users and it will seek evidence and proposals from service users more broadly. Such a Commission represents the first opportunity that citizens have had to shape and be part of the debate about the future of welfare state services as users of them.

> The Commission will provide an independent forum for discussion about the future of the welfare state: take the issue out of party politics, offer an effective way of getting service users' views, be consistent with the current aim of involving people in welfare instead of making decisions for them, and help inform the current debate. It will make possible a truly national and public discussion about the future of the welfare state and move it beyond the boundaries set by politicians and professionals.

The Commission will include and seek information from the key constituencies of welfare state service users, including older people, unemployed and other poor people, lone parents, carers, children and young people in care, recipients of mental health services, disabled people, people with learning difficulties and people with chronic illnesses.

The philosophy of the Commission

While the Commission's philosophy developed over the time it was established, it began with a clear set of principles. These included:

- valuing the views, ideas and proposals of welfare state service users;
- recognising the particular contribution which they can make because of the expertise they bring from their own experience;
- giving equal credibility to their perspective as to others;
- treating all welfare state service users with respect;
- reflecting this in the Commission's own working, so that welfare state service users involved in the Commission would always be treated with and treat each other with respect.

Setting up the Commission

The idea of the Commission came from Open Services Project, an independent user-led project concerned with increasing the say and control people have over services and agencies affecting their lives. This project already had a track record of work to increase service users' involvement in community care, social services and other areas of public policy. The two immediate priorities were to resource the Commission and to open up the process of decision-making about it. This reflected the twin priorities of putting the Commission on a secure footing and making sure that it functioned democratically.

As with setting up any innovatory initiative, the first big problem was getting *funding*. We decided to start with funding so that other service users would not be drawn unpaid into what might be a long drawn out and ultimately unsuccessful search for money. At the same time, we deliberately kept the detail of the Commission open and flexible, so that key decisions were not made before other welfare state service users were fully involved.

In the event our efforts to get funding took a long time, a lot of hard work and determination and nearly didn't succeed. We couldn't assume that funders would necessarily understand or be sympathetic to our objectives. One replied disingenuously, 'surely we are all users of the welfare state', as if the financially secure family which can make choices between private and state education or health care, is in the same position as someone facing long term unemployment, an older person without savings or an occupational pension, or a disabled person who requires full-time personal assistance to live independently. We wrote to the *Guardian* newspaper (11 November 1993) asking if it might be able to offer some support 'in view of the *Guardian's* particular recognition of the need to rethink welfare.' We did not receive a reply!

There was only a limited number of possible funders to which we could turn. The Nuffield Foundation, Joseph Rowntree

Foundation and Joseph Rowntree Charitable Trust all said the proposal fell outside their terms of reference. The Gulbenkian Foundation was supportive, but would only ever be able to offer partial funding and ultimately wasn't able to do that. The Baring Foundation finally did agree to fund us. The Foundation was supportive and helpful and treated our 'weaknesses' as strengths. Sadly, the subsequent collapse of the Baring Bank severely restricted the Foundation's resources and meant that we could not go back to them for any further funding as real costs became clearer, as often happens with such initiatives.

The Baring Foundation was our fourth attempt to secure funding and if this had failed there would probably have been nowhere else for us to turn. This is another indication of how precarious and uncertain the chances are for welfare state service users to contribute to debates about their futures. Sadly, the problem we faced appears to be far from unique. Initial research suggests that user-led initiatives like the Commission are disadvantaged when it comes to securing funding. (Barnes and Thompson, 1994)

Having very limited resources clearly restricted what we could do. It also made it important for our goals to be focussed and realistic so that we could set ourselves an achievable task. Nonetheless, as we have said, we believe that we have received evidence from more and a wider range of welfare state service users than any other inquiry into the welfare state and on service users' own terms.

Setting up a planning group

Once funding had been secured, the first step was to open up decision-making. This was done by recruiting a planning group, drawing on as wide a range of networks as possible to identify them. The planning group was made up of people from different parts of the country who were users of the welfare state and who also had experience of working together with other people. It included an older person, disabled person, person with learning difficulties, mental health service user, two lone parents on benefits and an unemployed person. The group had seven members: Zelda Curtis, Sally Fox, Marion Beales, Rose Thompson, Jackie Downer, Jane Campbell and Peter Beresford.

In all there were three meetings of the planning group over a period of seven weeks. At the first meeting, members of the group began by introducing themselves to each other, finding out more about the background of the Commission and then working out together what they wanted to do. They did this using a flip chart and reading out whatever was written down for those who could not read or see it. This was a technique which we also used later in the Commission itself. The first task people agreed on was for each person to say something about what they felt about the welfare state and 'our journey', trying to take the Commission forward: where they wanted to go, what goals they had and what outcomes they hoped for. These were some of the things people said:

At the end of the Commission, there is a move forward ... someone is listening or reading what comes out of it.

In this society childhood is meant to be special but in fact many children go without proper food. I want people to realise that we do want to get out of this situation, but to do that people need bridges ... I want an end to people being blamed.

To have a small success and be taken seriously. To look at our differences and see if there are any agreements. To look at what ordinary people mean by the welfare state and to get people's ideas about what it is and should be.

The planning group agreed that:

We must own this idea of the Commission for and by service users one hundred per cent and not let it get taken over and stolen. Our involvement in our issues is crucial and we can display to the world what this is all about. The reality of our vision of the welfare state is what we have to offer.

The overall task of the planning group was to work out what needed to be done and set the work of the Commission in train. The group focussed on three main tasks. These were:

- recruiting members of the Commission
- starting the process of recruiting a worker
- beginning to let welfare state service users know about the Commission.

Recruiting Commission members

We had funding to have twelve Commission members. The

planning group wanted to reflect the range of different welfare state service users as well as differences according to age, 'race', gender, sexual identity, disability and class in the Commission's membership. The planning group didn't want the Commission to be 'just a group or network of friends' or for it to 'end up competing over our different concerns, for example lone parents, competing with disabled people' and it wanted to 'be supportive if a member of the Commission needed support to play their full part in it'. We decided that the best way of getting a wide range of membership was by making contact with relevant organisations of service users which members of the planning group were in touch with and then make phone contact with a particular individual. In this way the process could be as inclusive as possible. The group worked out together a 'person specification' for members of the Commission, which included the qualities which we thought were important. These were

- a commitment to the Commission
- an interest in the future of the welfare state
- a sensitivity about and concern with other groups, not just your own 'group' or people in the same situation as yourself
- to have your own networks
- communication abilities
- interpersonal abilities
- ability to work as a member of a team
- willingness to travel
- experience as 'users' or recipients of welfare state services.

The planning group agreed that its members could go on to be members of the Commission if they wished to, but should not regard this as an obligation. In the event some people continued as members of the Commission, while others didn't. As a result of this process, the membership of the Commission included lone parents, disabled people, people on benefits and low income, carers, a mental health service user, student, person with learning difficulties and older person.

Recruiting the worker

We wanted to recruit the worker in as inclusive and 'equal opportunities' a way as possible. The usual practice in such projects of advertising in the *Guardian* and professional press would not be appropriate in this case and anyway we couldn't afford it. Instead we sought to use the newsletters, mailings and networks of organisations of people who use welfare state services and of associated voluntary organisations. *Big Issue* and *Disability Now* also offered us cheap advertising. We received more than 100 enquiries which resulted in 52 applications. These came from a wide range of welfare state service users, including lone parents, unemployed people, people on low wages, disabled people, mental health service users, older people and students. This vindicated our view that there would be welfare state service users both interested in and able to do such work. Members of the planning group worked out a job and person specification for the worker; that is to say the tasks which the worker would be expected to do and the skills and qualities which she would need to have. (see Appendix F) An essential qualification for the worker, as for members of the Commission, was that she/he had relevant experience as a user of welfare state services.

The planning group decided that the appointment of the worker should ultimately be the responsibility of the Commission, but that they should set the ball rolling so that members of the Commission could shortlist, interview and appoint the worker without unnecessary delay. This is what happened. Four of us drew up a shortlist of six from applicants with the necessary qualifications and then we interviewed them using the same agreed questions which related to the job and person specifications. Sadly the worker we appointed had to withdraw from the Commission some way into the job on grounds of ill health. As could be expected this created additional problems because of the Commission's limited resources. Fortunately we were then able to appoint the runner up for the job in his place, Michael Turner, who carried the work on to completion.

Letting people know about the Commission

From the start we knew that the Commission would be faced with a big problem in trying to reach welfare state service users. Many welfare state service users feel and indeed are isolated and excluded, for example through poverty, institutionalisation and restricted mobility. They are a difficult group to reach and this is compounded by the stigma associated with reliance on the welfare state which makes many people unwilling to admit to their situation. We also had the additional problem of very limited funding.

We also found ourselves subject to the same difficulties which the Commission sought to challenge and explore by involving service users in the debate about welfare. These seemed to be closely linked to the low value placed on what service users themselves have to say, existing hierarchies of credibility and prevailing news values.

For example, while the Commission's launch resulted in coverage in the specialist press and in service users' newsletters and magazines, there was no coverage in the national press or broadcast media. A crew from national TV news did not materialise at the launch as promised, in spite of their repeated confirmations. Subsequently, members of the Commission were contacted by ITN for an in-depth examination of poverty to mark the anniversary of the Jarrow Crusade. Five of us were recorded offering our views and analysis of poverty. This would have been the first time that people with experience of poverty would have had the chance to do this on UK television. However, the item was dropped at the last moment and we were phoned with apologies. The contribution from a right-wing academic arguing that there was no poverty in the UK, however, was retained. We have since discovered that this experience is a common one among user-led initiatives.

When we tried to get a slot on access TV to highlight the contribution of service users in debates about welfare, we couldn't. Instead a well known anti-welfare right-wing academic was given the one space the series was devoting to the welfare state, even though he had many other forums on which to present his well-known views. (Marsland, 1994)

We knew that limited media interest would restrict the number of welfare state service users we could hope to reach, but we still felt that it was important to take this essential first step.

Fortunately our efforts to get further funding did meet with one small success. *Community Care* magazine gave us a grant of £2,000 to produce and disseminate information and leaflets. Given our restricted resources we knew we could only hope to reach some welfare state service users and that we had to be realistic in our expectations. At the same time, we felt that the process of involving them had to start somewhere and that every welfare state service user we were able to reach represented another move forward. The recruitment of the worker was one of the first ways in which we raised the profile of the Commission and made contact with welfare state service users more generally. The other approaches which we used included:

- producing different leaflets for different constituencies, for example mental health service users and disabled people, and distributing them through their mailings and networks;
- distributing information about the Commission within our own local and national networks and contacts as individual members of the Commission;
- using mailings and networks of national and umbrella voluntary organisations;
- by word of mouth and through leaving leaflets and information in doctors' surgeries, meeting places, projects and on service users' and voluntary organisations' notice boards;
- through publicity received from the launch of the Commission in specialist and service users' journals and newsletters;
- by Commission members and supporters taking information and leaflets to meetings and conferences which they attended.

The Citizens' Commission

Commission members met for the first time on 1 February 1995. In all we met four times over a period of eighteen months. We did not have the funding to meet more often, but members also kept in contact and maintained their involvement through phone calls and letters. Each of our meetings was for half a day. We placed a particular emphasis on trying to work together in an effective, positive and supportive way. This was an objective which we established in the planning group and sought to maintain in the Commission itself. We gave this particular priority for two main reasons. First, we thought that the better we could work together the more we were likely to achieve. Second, welfare state service users, particularly people living on low income and with restricted choices, are likely to have a difficult and stressful life and it is important that any activities in which they are involved do not add to their difficulties, but instead represent something positive in their lives. Members of the Commission seemed to enjoy the meetings. The atmosphere was friendly, lively, enthusiastic and we also worked hard! Commission members showed enormous commitment, working hard to achieve its aims. But such an outcome is not achieved by chance or without effort. Together we agreed on a number of key principles and practices to help ensure that we worked positively and effectively together. These were good ideas which members of the Commission had learnt from other experience. Many were first adopted by the planning group for its working. These principles and practices included:

• **meeting people's expenses fully and appropriately**

Because users of welfare state services are often on low incomes and have additional demands on their finances, we gave priority to trying to meet all the costs they might incur by being involved in the Commission so that they would not be out of pocket. This included travelling and subsistence expenses, child care and personal assistance costs, any incidental expenses which might be incurred and costs for support. We also aimed to be flexible so that Commission members had the money they needed when they needed it. For example, they might need travelling expenses up-front, or immediately after their expenditure, or to be paid in cash because they didn't have a bank account. We were anxious to ensure that lack of money, and the stigma that frequently goes with it, would never be a problem for people as members of the Commission.

• **agreeing ground rules**

First in the planning group and then in the Commission itself, we identified and agreed a set of ground rules (see Appendix D) to govern our behaviour with each other and to provide a basis for behaving with respect and equality towards each other. Some of us already knew from experience that such ground rules can be helpful in ensuring that people are treated as equals and are able to participate fully. Our ground rules included, for example, ensuring that everyone had their say and not interrupting each other, treating any personal experience people might mention as confidential and for members to be able to take a break in meetings if and when they might need one.

• payment

The experience of using welfare state services is often devalued in our society. In the Commission we placed a particular value on it and wanted to reflect this in our working. We agreed that members of the planning group and the Commission should be paid for the work which they did as a token of recognition and respect for their knowledge, expertise and experience. Service users are often expected to make their contribution without recompense. We did not want to mirror this model. Members of the Commission were paid for their participation in meetings and for carrying out group discussions.

• equal opportunities policy

As part of our objective of working in as equal a way as possible, we formulated an equal opportunities statement as the basis for an equal opportunities policy. We drew on existing experience in voluntary organisations, (see Cheung-Judge and Henley, 1994) agreed a policy statement (see Appendix G) and took collective responsibility for equal opportunities policy. Equal opportunities issues cropped up on several occasions in the work of the Commission. For instance, at our first meeting when one member asked if there was 'anything we would want to exclude from (this) Report', it was agreed that 'any discriminatory statements that were, for example, racist or sexist' we would exclude. We talked about having ground rules for the (group discussions with welfare state service users) to ensure that there was 'respect for everybody' and we went on to produce these.(see Appendix G) When we talked about doing group discussions at our third meeting, when members had started to undertake them, we agreed that:

> if people persisted in making prejudiced and discriminatory remarks, after being asked not to, then we will end the discussion and leave.

Fortunately, in the event, this was not to be a problem.

• good quality conditions

As part of our commitment to making the work of the Commission a positive and enjoyable experience for its members, we aimed to provide a good quality working environment, meeting in pleasant surroundings and providing good quality refreshments. Our meetings began with a sandwich lunch, with a break later in the afternoon for hot and cold drinks and biscuits.

• access and support

We held the meeting of the Commission in a fully accessible meeting place. We also sought to identify and address other issues of access. For example, the Commission member from the self-advocacy organisation of people with learning difficulties, *People First*, usually came with a supporter, whose costs were also met. Information was provided for her in preferred form, which was audio-cassette tape. *People First* ask organisations with whom they work to sign up to a set of principles which they have found helpful to ensure equal and inclusive working and the Commission was happy to do this. (see Appendix E) We made sure that Commission meetings were not too long, especially for people who had had to travel a long way and, for example, that smokers could go out for a break when they needed to. We also sought individually and collectively to be supportive to each other informally, offering help, information and encouragement as we went along.

Taken together, all these measures helped to ensure that all members of the Commission were fully included on equal terms and could make their best contribution. We sought to avoid formal or informal hierarchies in how we worked and to develop our agenda and make decisions by agreement. While we certainly did not agree about everything, people behaved openly and with respect for each other. Respect was a key value underpinning the Commission. Just as its key objective was to demonstrate respect for welfare state service users by involving them in the debate about the future of welfare, so we sought to do the same in our own working with each other, reflecting the goals and aspirations of the Commission to involve people on equal terms. In the event one member of the Commission experienced increasing difficulties and pressures from social security and dropped out and we lost touch with another two thirds of the way through the work, when he got a job.

Working together

As well as trying to provide the conditions for us to work well together, we placed an emphasis on working things out together and making collective decisions. We did this in a number of way, including, for example:

- being clear about and agreeing our role as Commission members;
- trying to keep people in touch with what was happening;
- not making important decisions without consultation. This meant a lot of telephone calls, as well as letters to keep people posted, in addition to our meetings;
- agreeing work so that people could take on tasks they felt comfortable with.

For example, at the Commission's first meeting:

> *The question was raised as to what is expected of individual members and what will we do. It was agreed that it is for all of us to agree between us. Some people may want to have discussions only with other service users who are in the same position as themselves, for example as disabled people or carers, but people don't have to do that and may want to go and meet others.*

We worked out how we would carry out our work by discussion, brainstorming and using a flip chart. This was how we decided what our focus would be when we met with people and asked them for evidence. We agreed that:

> *It is important to look at what people want for themselves and their lives and not just at particular welfare state services like social services and benefits.*

This led to a discussion about what we meant by the welfare state and so we put up a flip chart, offering our individual ideas and agreeing our overall definition. The flip chart read:

The welfare state

Benefits and pensions
Transport
Support services/community care (including young and old people)
Housing
Child care
Employment
Taxes – how we pay them, who benefits and who pays
Education for children and adults

Leisure facilities
Environment

Discrimination: this is important because there has been a lot of discrimination in the welfare state and everyone has not been treated equally

The welfare state is also about:
* Being a full citizen
* Achieving your potential
* Having rights
* Knowing what you want to make that possible – to have a fuller life
* What you want for your life and what you want for the future.

Why 'welfare state'?

We decided to call the Citizens' Commission, the Commission on the Future of the Welfare State. This did not mean that we as a group necessarily signed up to or accepted all the meanings and traditions associated with the welfare state – far from it. We did not assume ourselves, or expect other welfare state service users to think, that welfare was necessarily a 'good thing' or that it was the most helpful way of meeting people's needs and safeguarding their rights. People on the receiving end of the welfare state's services, particularly its heavy-end policies and provisions for poor people, have good reason to question and challenge its paternalism and have first hand experience of its failings and limitations.

More generally there is also a desire among conventional policy and campaign organisations not to be tied to past concepts and terms in trying to develop policy for the future. For some, 'welfare state' is a term they have made a conscious decision not to use. For them it carries too much unhelpful baggage and political connotations.

But at the same time, it is a term which people more generally are familiar with. It has a powerful history and it means something to them. We may not all be talking about the same thing. We may not all have thought carefully about what it means to us or what we mean when we use the term. But it is a point of departure. It figures in popular discussions. For this reason we decided to use the term as

our starting point. We also made a decision to call ourselves
'*Citizens*' Commission'. When we first had the idea, we called it a
service users' commission. But people don't necessarily like to be
thought of in these terms and they may not want to use services at
all. So we decided instead on the term *citizens* because we felt it
conveyed the importance of people's rights and responsibilities
generally and in relation to the welfare state specifically.

How we did the work

As we have said, our aim in the Commission was to enable welfare state service users to offer their ideas, views and proposals and then to put them together, analyse them and produce a report as a basis for action. It is helpful to look at what we did as a *research* project. This offers a useful framework for explaining and describing the way we did the work. Such a research project entails a number of stages. These are:

- designing the research
- collecting information
- collating and analysing information
- writing up the research
- disseminating findings as a basis for making change.

Designing the research

There are two related aspects to designing research. These have to do with *why* you are doing it and *how* you are doing it: the research methodology and research methods. We will begin with the first of these.

Our approach to research

While we recognised that what we were doing was essentially carrying out a research project, we also knew that it was unlike most conventional research. It was based on a very different philosophy. Our research approach rested on two related methodologies. These were those of *participatory* and *emancipatory* research. At the heart of both are concerns to equalise relationships between the researcher and the subjects of research, to involve the subjects of research in the research process and to make change which benefits the subjects of research.

This kind of 'user-led' research methodology has been

developed by community organisations and organisations of social care service users and other subjects of social research and the service system, disillusioned with existing research models and their damaging effects on them. Alan Stanton has identified some of the characteristics of participatory research, while making clear that there is no one rigid model. He says:

> Participatory research recognises that most research serves the powerful: government over the governed; managements over workers. So its goal is democratic as well as collaborative inquiry. This means the core issue is empowerment: not only people's involvement, but their control. It challenges inequality by supporting people in the creation of their own knowledge: strengthening their abilities and resources. Its rationale is their right to participate actively in processes affecting their lives. Writers on participatory research often see this link between research and action as its characteristic feature. Investigation, analysis, learning and taking action, aren't separate and distinct, but an interrelated whole. Investigation may be initiated by outside researchers, but it should remain anchored in the issues of the community or workplace.
> *Stanton*, 1989, p332

According to Mike Oliver, the disability activist and writer, the two key fundamentals on which an emancipatory approach to research must be based:

> are empowerment and reciprocity. These fundamentals can be built in by encouraging self-reflection and a deeper understanding of the research process by the research subjects themselves as well as by enabling researchers to identify with their research subjects.
> *Oliver*, 1996, p141

There is now a growing body of such 'user-led' and emancipatory research. There are examples from organisations of disabled people, people with learning difficulties, psychiatric system survivors, people living with HIV/AIDS and other groups. This development represents a break with the tradition of one group of people studying and reporting on another, to people undertaking their own research, under their own control. It is being used to find out what service users want; to monitor and evaluate policy, practice and services. There is now more than enough experience to show that such participatory and emancipatory research is both possible and effective.

Its objectives of involvement and empowerment were at the heart of both how we worked together in the Commission and how we sought to carry out our work with welfare state service users. We worked out the 'whys' and 'hows' of carrying out our inquiry *together*. While the fact that people were undertaking their own research meant that it was different, it was not inferior. It was based on well established methods and carried out carefully and systematically.

Collecting information

Now we move on to how we carried out our inquiry. Because we had very limited resources we realised we could only reach some welfare state service users. But we wanted to include as wide a range of views as possible. We wanted to make it possible both for people who were actively involved in user groups and campaigns to offer their views and also people who were not involved in this way, but who were concerned and involved only as individuals. We also wanted to include people who were familiar with debates about welfare and those who weren't. We wanted to include people who had formulated demands and people who hadn't; people with high expectations and low expectations.

To achieve these objectives we decided on a two-fold approach to gaining welfare state service users' views. We would carry out a series of *group* discussions in different parts of the country and with different groups of service users and we would also encourage groups and particularly *individuals* to send us evidence themselves. We knew we could only undertake a certain number of group discussions. By inviting individuals to send their views we could widen the range of welfare state service users who could contribute and not be restricted only to those with whom we made direct contact and also ensure that there was a way of taking part available for more isolated individuals. Each method has its strengths and limitations, but together they make possible a fuller, more inclusive picture from welfare state service users.

What we asked people

We decided to devote time at the second meeting of the Commission to working out what we would ask welfare state service users. We spent some time brainstorming and writing our ideas up on a flip chart. These questions, with minor changes to ensure clarity and reliability and with some additions, were the basis for group discussions and the short questionnaires we produced for groups and individuals to give evidence. (see Appendix G)

Individual evidence

By seeking views and evidence from individuals, we hoped to make it possible for people who were not affiliated to organisations, or involved in self-help or support groups, to contribute too. Another strength which individual contributions are said to have, is that people can say things, particularly personal things, which they might be reluctant to mention in front of others. While this may be the case, in our experience participants in group discussions were also remarkably forthcoming about private, often intimate, experiences linked with welfare. We received information from individuals in letters, on tape, by telephone calls and through the short questionnaire leaflet that we distributed. A wide range of welfare state service users contributed in this way, including black and white people, older, disabled and unemployed people. In all we received evidence from 67 individuals.

Group discussions

While we relied on people contacting us for individual evidence, the group discussions made up the largest part of our work seeking evidence. In all we undertook 28 group discussions. We carried these out in two ways. First, members of the Commission organised and undertook discussions with groups that they were in contact with or knew of in their areas. In most cases these were discussions with groups who shared the same experience as them, for example as people with learning difficulties or carers. We made a deliberate decision to do this, to make the most of people's shared experience and also to avoid situations where there might be competing interests, for example, if non-disabled carers were to meet with disabled people. Not everyone felt they wanted to undertake discussions. One member of the Commission, for example, was reluctant to carry out discussions with groups she knew because, as she said, their view was that initiatives like the Commission would not have any effect. Members respected her wishes.

The second part of our strategy was to identify priority groups which were not represented by Commission members, and also to talk to people in parts of the country not covered by members of the Commission. This enabled us to meet with welfare state service users in England, Scotland and Wales and in urban and rural areas. We did not carry out any discussions in Northern Ireland but we did receive enquiries and evidence from there. Our priority groups were those whose views we thought it was particularly important to obtain because they are often overlooked and experience particular exclusion. The Commission worker was responsible for carrying out this work. The groups we identified included:

- young people aged 16–18 excluded from receiving benefits
- black and minority ethnic groups
- people working for low pay
- homeless people
- people living with HIV/AIDS
- drug users
- teenage mothers
- people with child care responsibilities.

Group discussions have particular strengths. They give participants the chance to develop their thoughts and ideas, bounce ideas off each other and take their discussion forward. They help give people the confidence to say what they want, which comes from having each others' support. For these reasons this method of gaining people's views and ideas was particularly consistent with the participatory goals of the Commission.

We decided not to have discussions with groups or projects which claimed to represent service users, but which were not controlled by them, for example social services departments and large charities for disabled people, although we did include service users brought together by such organisations. To reach the different groups and areas which we had prioritised required a more structured approach than when members of the Commission undertook their own discussions. We used a snowball approach, starting with existing networks, which then led us to other national and local contacts. As well as identifying and contacting organisations linked specifically with our priority groups, we also contacted wider groups and projects like community and drop-in centres.

We discovered that while the voluntary sector is large, many non-service provider organisations are not in direct contact with service users or able to put people in touch with them. Also, while it was not difficult, for example, to reach groups of lone parents and disabled people, there seemed to be few groups organised around the welfare state or issues like unemployment.

Carrying out the group discussions highlighted the broader problems of reaching welfare state service users and involving them in the discussion about it. It takes time, effort and determination. It requires considerable skill and sensitivity. Reaching welfare state service users was a difficult and sometimes frustrating task. We estimate that to reach the groups who took part in the inquiry, we contacted more than 100 by letter and phone. We also produced and distributed thousands of leaflets and questionnaires.

We tried to support welfare state service users' participation in the Commission by meeting all their expenses so that, for example, child care responsibilities, lack of personal assistance or of accessible transport, would not prevent them taking part or put them out of pocket. We went to see them rather than expecting them to come to us and met the cost of meeting places and refreshments where this was needed. But there were also other important obstacles in the way of welfare state service users' participation in the Commission. This was apparent from the reasons which groups gave who did *not* want to take part.

These reasons fell into three categories: they were too busy, they didn't see any point or they weren't interested. The first two categories are of particular significance. The groups who *did* take part were often small, fragile, overstretched and tied up with their own activities. This meant that frequently when they met with us, they were busy and had to break off from what they were doing. But the response of welfare state service users and their organisations also seemed to be shaped by what they thought could be achieved. Many conveyed a strong sense of powerlessness. It was clear that they doubted that service users or the Commission could make much impact on the future of welfare. Some asked us, 'What can it achieve? What will happen with it?' This was not said in a dismissive way, but out of concern about what difference the Commission could make and whether it was just a paper exercise. Our response was that the Commission might achieve a little and that if we didn't do it, welfare state service users wouldn't even have had a chance to have a say. If they had that chance, it couldn't be said in the future that nobody knew what welfare state service users had to say and what they wanted. Similarly some of the individuals and groups we contacted also felt initially that they might not have anything to say or contribute, although as we shall see, taking part in the Commission generally proved them wrong. Motivating welfare state service users to take part in the Commission was not always easy. The strong sense of disempowerment which many conveyed can be seen as part of a vicious circle which perpetuates and reinforces their exclusion. We particularly wanted to include in group discussions people who lived in residential homes and in another day centre. When we tried, however, service users were reluctant to get involved, so sadly we were unable to include some of those most reliant on the welfare system because they were wary of taking part.

When the Commission tried to arrange discussions in residential homes and in a day centre there was not sufficient interest amongst people to proceed. These people probably represent some of those who are most dependent on the state, but they appear to believe that their opinions have no importance.

Carrying out the group discussions

Group discussions can be difficult and demanding to do. The two-way nature of the situation and the greater equality of the relationship compared to one-to-one research interviews encourages this. Some members of the Commission had been involved in initiatives like the Commission before. Others had not and had not carried out any research themselves. The planning group had deliberately not made such experience a requirement of our person specification for Commission members, as it felt that this would unnecessarily restrict membership. It believed instead that members could be *supported* to gain such skills. This is one of the lessons of user-led research, and it worked for the Commission. We put together information and support for people to carry out group discussions and spent time talking about it at one of our meetings. We also kept in touch with Commission members, offering information and guidance when it was needed. They were able to gain new skills and new confidence from doing research. We also produced ground rules for the discussions to help ensure participants' confidentiality and a safe environment. (see Appendix G)

One group of very young people seemed unwilling to say much. In some cases only some people who were present wanted to take part in the discussion. Initially some of those who did participate were reluctant to talk. Some were nervous about going on record, for example one individual was concerned about the tape recorder. But once the discussion began, generally everyone who took part would contribute. Participants had a lot to say. They had ideas about how things could be improved as well as criticisms to make of existing arrangements. Both the worker and members of the Commission who undertook group discussions emphasised the openness and honesty of participants. The discussions seemed to be a positive and empowering experience for both participants in the group discussions and the people who carried them out.

This relates to one of the principles underlying the Commission: that the trust, empathy, understanding and shared experience which comes from a 'user-led' approach to an inquiry about welfare would generate fuller, more candid and reliable information. As one member of the Commission, who had never undertaken any research before, said:

> It was important to the people that I spoke to that I was in the same boat as them. I wasn't just another academic or professional, that I wouldn't talk down to them, but I actually knew about their experience first hand and could understand it.

This may help explain why people seemed to take us so much into their confidence. In contrast, one of the reasons why some people were reluctant to get involved was because of their negative experiences of conventional research, saying, for example: 'We've bloody been surveyed. We're fed up with it.' We don't believe that people would have shared with us some of the things which they said if our relationship with them was not as equal as it was.

A frequent concern expressed about initiatives and studies which seek to involve service users is that their participants are 'unrepresentative'. This is sometimes used to discredit or devalue their activities and findings. (Beresford and Campbell, 1994) We make no claim that the Commission was a quantitative research project based on a random sample of people. It wasn't intended to be such and clearly wasn't. But at the same time, we sought to include as wide a range of people and perspectives as possible and with some exceptions, for example, travellers and Deaf people, we succeeded. As we have said, we also sought to address issues of difference according to 'race', gender, sexual identity, disability, age and class. There seemed to be a significant degree of consistency in what people said. For example, groups of young people from different parts of the country and groups of much older people from the home counties both had similar proposals to offer for funding welfare for the future.

The groups ranged widely in size: there were 35 in one and just two in another! Mostly they ranged from about six to 12 people, which made a manageable and comfortable size for discussion. Mixed groups were generally balanced according to gender. In addition to the groups specifically of black and Asian people, some of the other groups also included black people. Discussions generally lasted between 45 minutes and an hour.

Different groups had their own particular concerns and raised these in the discussions. For example, lone parents were worried about the Child Support Agency and people living with HIV/AIDS were concerned about the availability of treatment that was available. The pressure on people in their day to day lives to focus on issues which specifically affected them, meant that they often had had less time to think about broader welfare issues. The Commission both raised the issue of the need to connect particular issues affecting different groups of welfare state service users with broader ones and began to address it. While some discriminatory comments were made, for example about drug users getting services and 'immigrants' 'coming and getting benefits', this was uncommon.

Analysing and collating the evidence

If collecting information is a big job, then pulling it together is always an even bigger one. When we had finished gathering evidence, we had a pile of transcriptions more than a foot high, a thick sheaf of completed questionnaires and three files of enquiries and submitted evidence.

We used a two-stage approach to analysing and collating the information we gathered. This reflected the participatory goals of the project. First the worker began the process of analysing information.

Then when he had identified key issues from it, we used these as the basis for discussion at the fourth and final meeting of the Commission. The aim was to enable members of the Commission collectively to offer their views and analysis of the findings. This discussion was tape recorded. Members of the Commission who could not be at the meeting also contributed their views through telephone interviews, which were written down in full. These discussions also formed a basis for the Commission's proposals and recommendations. There was an important collaborative dimension to collation and analysis in the Commission. As far as we know, this is the first time that this has been done.

Writing up the Commission's work

Our worker had lead responsibility for writing up the findings of the Commission, while the convener, who had been involved from the beginning, was primarily responsible for the introductory chapters. The Report of the findings went through a process of redrafting. A regret which we had was that we did not send transcripts back to groups for them to correct and change or a first draft of the Report. But we had neither time nor resources to do this. What we did do however was provide a copy of the final Report for all groups who took part in the Commission.

In keeping with the participatory philosophy underpinning this project, in both analysing and collating information and writing the book, we sought to reflect the issues and priorities raised by participants, rather than impose our own categories on what they said and group them together according to some system of our own. This is an approach which is known as 'grounded theory', that is to say, one which builds on participants' own analysis and ideas rather than fitting them into some pattern preset by the analyst or researcher.

One consequence of this is that we have organised material according to policies and themes offered by welfare state service users, rather than divided them simply on the basis of their views about existing provision and their proposals for the future. While this might have been a simpler and more conventional way of presenting their views, it would not have corresponded to the way in which they were offered or reflected their trains of thought.

Making change

The usual approach to bringing about change, when new knowledge or information is obtained about a social issue or problem, is to seek media coverage and to try and influence politicians and policy makers at local and central government levels. While we did not ignore this approach and regarded it as important to gain mainstream media coverage and to inform politicians and policy makers, we did not see this as the main way in which we hoped to influence debates and developments about welfare.

We recognised at an early stage that the amount of interest we could expect following this route would be limited for an initiative like the Commission. We had little chance of bringing about change through conventional mass media/parliamentary methods. Not only do large pressure groups and voluntary organisations have limited success doing this, but we also saw reports on the future of welfare by other organisations much more powerful than us, being lost without trace. (for example, Transport and General Workers Union, 1994; Yarrow, 1995) During the life of the Commission, we also saw the high profile (Milne, 1995) report of the Commission on Social Justice set aside by the Labour Party. We therefore could not assume that a conventional approach would work for us, whether or not it worked for others.

Our experience from involvement in service users', community and disabled people's organisations and movements led us to another approach, which they have pioneered. This is one based much more on a model of 'bottom-up' rather than 'top-down' change. At the Commission's third meeting we said:

> It is possible for us to be different. It could be a good idea to seek the support of our different organisations ... We are not a powerful group in conventional terms, but the Report could be useful and helpful for local and national campaigning if groups have access to it, to support what they want to do, and the Report has support from as many groups and organisations as possible. We agreed we would try and do this.
>
> NOTES OF MEETING, 20 JUNE 1995, p3

We therefore viewed the production of the Commission's Report as part of a longer term strategy of dissemination particularly focussed on grassroots organisations. We placed our priority on informing and supporting discussion and campaigning on the welfare state among and between welfare state service users' groups, organisations and movements at local and national levels. Spreading the word among 'ourselves' seemed a feasible and achievable objective, which could provide a basis for wider action as well as accessing and exchanging ideas and information among welfare state service users and their organisations. In this way we hoped that the efforts of individuals and groups of welfare state service users who took part in the Commission would have a real chance of serving a positive purpose as a resource for others.

Not the last word

We see this Report as a beginning, not an end. We feel that the Commission has achieved its first objective. It has given some welfare state service users an opportunity to say what they think and what they want, and generally participants seem to have valued this. But it is just a first and modest stage in making it possible for everyone who uses welfare state services to say what they would like to see for the future. As we said at the beginning of this Report, we aren't suggesting that the Commission is the last word on what service users have to say about welfare. Instead we hope it will signal the start of much more discussion along similar lines. It has necessarily been a modest project. We couldn't get money to do more than that. But it has enabled more welfare state service users than ever before to say what they would like to see for the future. It's the first word in what we hope will be a much bigger discussion.

PART 2

What service users say about welfare

Welfare state and welfare benefits: Present and future

In this Chapter we focus on what service users had to say about the welfare state and welfare benefits. This includes both their comments on their experience of existing benefits provision and their ideas and proposals for the future. It is a substantial chapter because benefits raise many issues and pose many problems for welfare state service users.

Service users' views about the welfare state

We wanted to find out more about people's views and ideas about welfare generally: what they thought of it and what it meant to them. We asked them what they thought were the good and bad things about the welfare state. Most people struggled when we asked them what they thought the good things were. Many said 'none'. Participants offered a wide range of comments:

> *What welfare state? I don't think there is one anymore.*
> GROUP OF PEOPLE ON LOW INCOME, WALES

> *The only good point is it stops people from starving.*
> AFRO-CARIBBEAN GROUP, MIDLANDS

> *Nothing! Not a single thing.*
> LESBIAN MOTHERS GROUP, GLASGOW

> *It's better than the workhouse – but that's where we're going to end up.*
> GROUP OF LONE PARENTS, WALES

> *The question is: is there a welfare state now?*
> GROUP OF PEOPLE ON LOW INCOME, WALES

> *There's nothing I can honestly say is good about.*
> GROUP OF LONE PARENTS, GLASGOW

Privatisation and tight budgets have led to financial considerations being put before people's needs.
WOMAN, KENT (25)

Lack of support, shortage of hospital beds, unfair system of benefits...
WOMAN, KENT (12)

With some prompting, participants did suggest some positives. These tended to be basic gains which the welfare state offered, which might perhaps be taken for granted; for example:

(Look at) a country which hasn't got a welfare state and you have to pay every time you go to the doctor and you need expensive insurance to be able to have an operation ... I think it's good that we do get most of our medical care free.
GROUP OF CARERS, YORKSHIRE (D)

It's put a roof over my head and given me food.
GROUP OF EX-DRUG USER PARENTS, SHEFFIELD

We've still got something, it is salvageable.
GROUP OF UNEMPLOYED WOMEN, GLOUCESTERSHIRE

I do appreciate the fact that it's there. It's just you're made to feel very small for using it and it's so difficult to get the services you require.
GROUP OF EX-DRUG USERS, SHEFFIELD

Most of the traditional welfare state is good. It only needs re-tuning to modern circumstances.
MALE MENTAL HEALTH SERVICE USER RECEIVING BENEFITS, SHEFFIELD (28)

People who completed the Commission's questionnaire seemed to find it easier to identify parts of the system which they valued, with most citing benefits and the health service as the areas that were most important to them. Education was also mentioned by a high proportion of respondents. Several people said that although they do not use the welfare state at present, they valued the fact that it was there if they become unemployed or unable to work.

The negative experiences of many of the welfare state service users who took part in the discussion groups seemed to overshadow what people might value about the welfare state. To provide a check on this to help people focus on what they might value in the current system, we asked an additional question: What would it be like without the welfare state? Responses to this included:

There would not be a life without the welfare state.
GROUP OF TEENAGE MOTHERS, EDINBURGH

There would be lots of suffering without a welfare state. There would be no day centres, no benefits, no hospitals, no doctors.
GROUP OF PEOPLE WITH LEARNING DIFFICULTIES, LONDON

There would be a higher crime rate, people would be stealing to survive.
GROUP OF TEENAGE MOTHERS, EDINBURGH

Participants believed that the effects of losing the welfare state would be extreme poverty accompanied by crime and civil unrest.

What the welfare state means to people

Most of the people who we spoke to and who sent in their views focused on the benefits system as the main part of the welfare state. However, it became clear as discussions developed that welfare state service users saw benefits as just one part of an overall system, with issues around health and education clearly being tied in with financial support and income maintenance. For example:

It's not just benefits, it's the NHS, help for elderly people ...
GROUP OF DISABLED PEOPLE, COVENTRY

I think its a combination of them all ... benefits, the NHS, houses and social services. They should all work together.
GROUP OF OLDER PEOPLE, WOKING

My interpretation of the welfare state is everything to do with benefits, the monetary side of things. I wouldn't really have thought of the NHS as welfare, but I can see there could be a more comprehensive approach, and perhaps it would be better if there was one and we should all be clearer about this.
GROUP OF PEOPLE LIVING WITH HIV/AIDS, MANCHESTER

It covers education, social services, provision of care, it's not just benefits ... if you got rid of one it has a knock on effect, a domino effect.
GROUP OF UNEMPLOYED WOMEN, GLOUCESTERSHIRE

It's to look after the less privileged in society. Everybody needs it at some time, we all need hospitals with doctors and what have you, but the less privileged you are, the more likely you are to need it.
GROUP OF CARERS, YORKSHIRE (D)

I could have paid for the treatment when I had my first heart attack because I had money through working, but if I had a relapse now and had to go to a paid hospital, I couldn't pay.
GROUP OF PEOPLE ON LOW INCOME, WALES

Short or long-term problem?

One of the issues which people's comments raise is whether the problems and shortcomings of the welfare state are the result of recent cuts and reforms or are more fundamental in origin. There didn't seem to be agreement about this among participants. But the views of welfare state service users appear to offer little comfort either to old left or new right. Right-wing reforms appear to have solved little and made many things worse. At the same time, it cannot be assumed that the welfare state initially got it right and was widely regarded as satisfactory by its recipients. For example:

It has certainly got worse, there's no doubt about it, but I do remember my mother saying the same things about the system a long time ago. I remember how she used to queue for hours and hours to get her benefit. I don't think it's ever been right.
GROUP OF PEOPLE ON LOW INCOME, WALES

It started to erode when Thatcher took over. In my day it was not bad, but then Thatcher took over.
GROUP OF CARERS, YORKSHIRE (A)

The welfare state services are now targetting specific groups and discriminating against these groups, for example single parents, young people and elderly. It is no longer caring. I am a black woman, one of the people discriminated against. I have had to work very hard to be where I am despite the education system failing me.
BLACK WOMAN, NOTTINGHAM (27)

THE BENEFITS SYSTEM

We now move to welfare state service users' comments about specific services. We begin with the benefits system: the area of welfare to which most resources are devoted and on which most discussion has so far concentrated. Participants in our inquiry also had much to say about benefits. They raised issues about the level of benefits; the 'benefits trap' and the way in which the system is actually administered. We will look at each of these in turn.

1. The inadequacy of the system

Everyone who gave evidence to the Commission condemned the level of benefits and pensions as inadequate. Critics may argue that 'they would say that wouldn't they'. But equally who would have a better understanding of how the benefits system actually worked than people on the receiving end? Welfare state service users' detailed comments raise two important issues. First, they highlight the *degree* of deprivation experienced by many people reliant on benefits. Second, they offer a direct challenge to the view that people claim and stay on benefits because they want to and because it is easy to live off the benefits system. Living on benefits is clearly anything but easy. For example:

> *You don't live on the benefit they're giving. You just exist on it.*
> GROUP OF UNEMPLOYED WOMEN, GLOUCESTERSHIRE

> *There's a furniture recycling project. The furniture's not in good condition, but there's nowhere else people can go for necessities like beds and tables and chairs. People go there and stand and wait for the vans to come in. It's awful that this has got to happen in this day and age.*
> GROUP OF PEOPLE ON LOW INCOME, WALES

> *I am constantly struggling to keep up with bills and end up robbing Peter to pay Paul all the time.*
> GROUP OF DISABLED PEOPLE, YORKSHIRE

> *What they're giving you at the moment wouldn't keep anyone for any length of time.*
> AFRO-CARIBBEAN GROUP, MIDLANDS

> *There's a misconception that everyone on benefit gets full entitlement to everything, but that's not true. A lot of people are paying full rent or full council tax or prescriptions.*

Paying the electricity – that's a problem for me – and the gas keeps coming to cut me off.
GROUP OF UNEMPLOYED WOMEN, GLOUCESTERSHIRE

People will be starving in the end because they've cut back the benefits so much, and you just haven't got enough money for the next week if your money hasn't come.
GROUP OF PEOPLE ON LOW INCOME, WALES

Even something as commonplace as watching television can become a struggle:

We have to hide away every time the TV detector van comes round, but it's our only form of enjoyment. People on low incomes and senior citizens should be able to get a cheap TV license.
LONE PARENT, YORKSHIRE (36)

The point raised by this individual reflects concern expressed by other participants that the current system for detecting license fee dodgers unfairly focuses on unemployed people and people with child care responsibilities who are at home in the day-time, as detector vans do not operate during 'unsocial hours' when people who do have jobs and are more likely to have the money to pay the fee are more likely to be watching television.

Benefits: concerns of specific groups

The benefits system includes a range of provision for specific groups of people, such as lone parents, disabled and older people. As might be expected, much of what people had to say about benefits and pensions related to the specific parts of the system that related to them.

Problems for parents

Parents, particularly lone parents, had a range of comments to make about the inadequacy of support for people who are bringing up children. For example, they said:

The benefits we get are rubbish ... I don't think the welfare state considers how much it actually costs a single parent to bring up kids on their own. They try to take more away from us and I don't think they've got their facts right.

If you have three children they expect you to live on only £85, you've got bills to pay, you've food to buy, clothes to buy for the kids, it just

isn't a lot, so you can actually be standing on the street and you haven't even got the bus fare home. I mean, the government says that single mothers only have kids to have an easy time of it and all that, but it's a load of rubbish.
GROUP OF LONE PARENTS, GLASGOW

It's bloody difficult, as I've still got endowments to pay (on a mortgage) which the government doesn't take into account. And there's still everything that goes with having a house.
LESBIAN MOTHERS GROUP, GLASGOW

Everybody seems to think that because you're a one parent family you get more Income Support, but it's not at all true because you've got more to pay and what you pay is going up and up. I've got to pay for school trips, which you never used to, but I can't always afford £5 to send my little girl on trips with the rest of them.
GROUP OF UNEMPLOYED PEOPLE, YORKSHIRE

Lone parents had particularly scathing comments to make about the role played by the Child Support Agency:

They do not check up right to find out if (they know) the right amount this person is bringing in.
GROUP OF LONE PARENTS, YORKSHIRE

Fathers have to pay now but you don't get anything extra, in fact, you're penalised if you don't give the father's name, and there's no way I can do that safely.
GROUP OF LONE PARENTS, WALES

Teenage mothers have been the focus of considerable condemnation by those who argue that the welfare state creates a 'dependency culture' and is abused by those who do not want to work or contribute to society. This criticism has perpetuated a stereotype of teenage women deliberately becoming pregnant in order get housing and a higher level of benefit. The reality for women in this situation is very different. As teenage mothers themselves said:

We're not given enough money to get by on ... When you're under 16 you don't get much. Just £8.45 for you and the child.
GROUP OF TEENAGE MOTHERS, EDINBURGH

I have to go without the bare essentials in life, and so does my son.
GROUP OF TEENAGE MOTHERS, LINCOLNSHIRE

We just get by on the basics – food, gas, electricity and that's it.
GROUP OF TEENAGE MOTHERS, EDINBURGH

Problems for young people

Young people more generally talked about their harsh treatment by
the benefits system. Those between the ages of 16 and 18 are
virtually excluded from the system. They are not entitled to Income
Support and can only get money through an emergency loans
system. As a group of young people told us, to get an emergency
loan the Benefits Agency:

*writes to your parents to get them to say they kicked you out, but my
parents would never say that. This can take over a week, but you
can die in 12 hours on the street, never mind waiting for the dole
office to write to your parents and them to write back.*
GROUP OF YOUNG PEOPLE FROM UK

Young people who were old enough to qualify for benefits
expressed similar views to other groups about the inadequacy of
benefit. For instance:

The welfare state means poverty. It just keeps you at poverty level.

*I find it hard to understand how the benefits are worked out. They
say you haven't got a job and they will give you x amount of money
to get the bare essentials. But they don't allow you heating –
everybody else has heating and just because we're unemployed it
doesn't mean we don't get cold, it's stupid. They seem to think you
can get by on food and that's it.*

*I've literally starved and lost weight. I've been so poor I couldn't
afford to eat and I couldn't afford to pay rent.*

*I go without completely ... I've got bills to pay and all those things,
and I have to go without food if I need a pair of shoes or something
like that. I have to go without for a long, long time to get things like
that. I have to live without the bare essentials, and my son does too
– not as much as I do, but more than enough. At the end of the day
the money that I'm living on is not enough for a single person these
days.*

*I was six-and-a-half months pregnant and they stopped my money
for a month.*

They don't just make it impossible to live comfortably, they make it

impossible to live. Especially if you're under 18. I'm out of that situation now, but I really do sympathise with those going through it now. I would never, ever want to go through that again. That was the worst possible time of my life, yet it's meant to be the best time of your life.
GROUP OF YOUNG PEOPLE FROM UK

Students are another group of young people who experience increasing problems of poverty and whose access to the benefits system has been reduced over time. Evidence submitted on behalf of a group of students reflected general concern about declining support for students, with broader consequences for the future:

Our grant system is a disgrace. Dramatic cuts have been made to the grants, but they have put the loan up. Lucky us! We're trying to make our lives better than we've been used to, but we're going to be paying thousands back when we graduate, and probably keeping our families on the breadline while we do so.

Some of our parents pay a parental contribution, meaning that they are forced to pay towards their 'child's' education. Their 'child' could be as old as 24. In everything else we are grown up at 16 or 18, but in college we are not mature until we are 21, which means our parents may still be making parental contributions when we are finishing a course at 24 years old.

Millions of people are unable to find jobs, but we are expected to find work during the three-month summer break. We are forced to this because we are not entitled to welfare benefits in the 22 weeks we are not at college.

Even whilst at college we are forced to do part-time jobs or night shifts. This doesn't exactly leave us bright-eyed and bushy-tailed for our studies.
WOMAN STUDENT, LANCASHIRE (10)

Problems for older people

Pensions were also criticised for their inadequacy by older people, who were also critical of the inadequacy of the state pensions they received. Many felt particularly hurt and disadvantaged at what they received, after paying into the system for all their working lives:

My pension is inadequate to cover the necessities of life – not luxuries – just so I can have a decent lifestyle.
GROUP OF OLDER WOMEN, LONDON

If you compare our pensions with other countries in Europe they are woefully inadequate and are barely enough to keep people at subsistence level. It shouldn't be necessary for people to go and get other benefits. Pensions are just being diluted and diluted and becoming worth less and less.
GROUP OF OLDER PEOPLE, WOKING

I've worked all my life and paid my stamp (National Insurance), so I haven't anything on top of my basic pension. So I just have £71 a week to pay my rent, gas, electric and telephone, which takes up about half my income, and then I have to buy food. I just don't get clothes and shoes and things like that which I need.
GROUP OF DISABLED PEOPLE, YORKSHIRE

Some older people said that they thought pension levels were reasonable and enough to get by on, but other members of the same groups challenged this and then it became clear that people had been talking about their private or occupational pensions. Older people were also very concerned about being penalised for having savings:

I've got enough money and that's from working. It's all been moved now because you can't get money from them if you've got money in the bank. I find it wrong. I worked all my life and was fortunate to do so, I shouldn't have to suffer when I give up work.
GROUP OF CARERS, YORKSHIRE (B)

I've got a small private pension and that just puts me over the limit where I could claim anything.
GROUP OF CARERS, YORKSHIRE (A)

People are penalised for being thrifty when they come just above the threshold for benefits and services. If you're below the threshold your standard of living can be quite a bit higher.
GROUP OF OLDER PEOPLE, WOKING

My husband was on a low income all his life but has paid into a pension scheme, then, when you retire, they penalise you for it.
GROUP OF CARERS, YORKSHIRE (B)

Pensions were also a concern for people contemplating their future. People we spoke to who were approaching retirement, were concerned about the pensions they would receive:

> Now I am coming near to pension age I feel that promises the welfare state has made in the past are gradually being whittled away. Soon there will be no welfare state left and my 40-45 years of contributions will have just gone to nothing.
>
> GROUP OF ASIAN DISABLED PEOPLE, LONDON

Problems for people living with HIV/AIDS

Some of these problems were highlighted by the group who took part in a discussion:

> It's increasingly difficult for people with HIV to access benefits. A few years ago more people died more quickly from the infection because there was less medical help available and so they were viewed as being 'properly disabled'. Now that many of us are living longer and getting more medical help and have a better quality of life, there are limits to the benefits that are paid. That means you don't get the disability benefits until you are really quite ill, although you still have needs. For example, many of us vary in size after periods of illness and having to keep buying things can really put a strain on your finances.
>
> The social security system is prejudiced towards gay people. I moved into Manchester because it's a less prejudiced area than where I used to live and me and my partner have applied for a community care grant to get set up. The adjudication officer said we should not get the grant because we moved into Manchester to be closer to the gay community. That should have nothing whatsoever to do with it. Then, on the other hand, the social security system sees us as cohabiting while we cannot be married legally.
>
> GROUP OF PEOPLE LIVING WITH HIV/AIDS, MANCHESTER

Problems for carers

The benefits system also includes a range of specific provisions for disabled people and for people who provide unpaid support for older and disabled people and mental health service users, as partners, family members and loved ones. People with such responsibilities felt particularly neglected by the system which they saw themselves as saving huge sums of money because they provided support instead of this being provided by formal services. For example:

I get Income Support and, honestly and truthfully, I do not smoke, I do not go out, I only buy my clothes from charity shops, and I can't manage.
GROUP OF CARERS, YORKSHIRE (D)

That Invalid Care Allowance is a total waste of time, I don't know why they even introduced it. It's meant to help if you stay home to look after your mother, daughter, sister, brother or whoever's got a disability, but if you're on social security it's deducted from the benefit you would be getting anyway, so where's the help in that? It's no help, it's just giving with one hand and taking back with the other.
AFRO-CARIBBEAN GROUP, MIDLANDS

If you give up work to be a carer like I've done, it rules out all the pension, because you can't make any contributions: you get Invalid Care Allowance, which is pathetic for caring full time, I mean, it's less than one pound an hour.
GROUP OF CARERS, YORKSHIRE (D)

Problems for disabled people

Disabled people have been hit by the introduction of the Incapacity Benefit, which replaced Invalidity Benefit in 1994. Restrictions are being placed on eligibility and disabled people are being subjected to additional tests. As members of one group of disabled people said:

The government is saying people are not sick or disabled with the new tests to qualify for Incapacity Benefit, so people will lose out because of the change.
GROUP OF ASIAN DISABLED PEOPLE, LONDON

Why the benefit system is inadequate

Participants had their own explanations for why the benefits system failed to meet their needs:

They are not tailored to the individual, they're tailored to the mass, so that doesn't help individual situations, so I think they try and make the lowest common denominator and give the minimal amount of money that they can give you.
LESBIAN MOTHERS GROUP, GLASGOW

Some simply saw the system as inflexible:

> I think we didn't get (the Cold Weather Allowance) because my son
> was over five. We're still single parents and still had a really, really
> cold house. Kids over five need the same amount of heating as those
> under five.
> LESBIAN MOTHERS GROUP, GLASGOW

Others believed that the system was inherently unfair in the way it
treated people. It was inequitable and inconsistent:

> They give with one hand and take with the other. You get Child
> Benefit and Family Credit but it hardly covers school dinner money.
> AFRO-CARIBBEAN GROUP, MIDLANDS

> I really dislike the way you can have two families living next door, in
> the same circumstances, but not getting the same money.
> GROUP OF PEOPLE ON LOW INCOME, WALES

People who owned their own home felt that benefit changes relating
to payments for their mortgages had created an unfair disparity
between home owners and people in rented accommodation, which
would deter people from taking out mortgages:

> If you have council accommodation your rent is paid immediately you
> go on benefits, but if you've got a mortgage there's a qualifying
> period.
> GROUP OF LONE PARENTS, WALES

> They say you should get insurance for your mortgage in case you
> lose your job, but the insurance company says you have to be
> earning £170 a week or more, so what can people do?
> AFRO-CARIBBEAN GROUP, MIDLANDS

Benefits and crime

The link between crime, benefits and unemployment has been the
subject of much political and media debate. One view which has
gained much credibility is that the benefits system encourages
'dependency' and perpetuates a dangerous 'underclass', generating
crime, social breakdown and disorder. People who spoke to the
Commission offered a very different picture of what was happening.
They said clearly and frankly that the *inadequacy* of benefits was
pushing people into crime in order to live.

A group of teenage mothers from Edinburgh thought that without the welfare state people would have to steal to survive. When we asked whether this happens at present, their reply was a clear 'Aye'. Comments from other participants gave a clear indication of knowledge of, if not actual involvement in, crime because of the inadequacy of benefits:

> They want to fight crime, but they can't win because they don't understand why people commit crime.
> GROUP OF YOUNG PEOPLE FROM UK

> There's people fiddling their gas, there's people fiddling the electric, there's people watching TV without a license.
> GROUP OF PEOPLE ON LOW INCOME, WALES

> If your Giro's not paid on Saturday, you've got to wait until Monday, and that's how people end up stealing and end up in jail.
> GROUP OF EX-DRUG USER PARENTS, SHEFFIELD

> People don't have enough money to live on, to pay their rent and gas and electric ... then they (other people) wonder why there's so many people in prison. It would be better if they tried to sort people out ... they just end up paying to keep people in prison.
> GROUP OF EX-DRUG USERS, SHEFFIELD

THE BENEFITS SYSTEM: THE FUTURE

In most of the groups who took part in the Commission, welfare state service users believed that there needed to be a basic change in the system used to decide who gets what support. They argued that this system needed to become more flexible so that it could respond more sensitively and effectively to people's actual needs. For example:

> I think what they should do is work out exactly how much a single parent with x number of children has, what you realistically need, and then base it on that ... and actually take into account that children need clothes, and shoes – just basic stuff that you need to live and to be the same as everybody else.
> LESBIAN MOTHERS GROUP, GLASGOW

Many participants also saw the inadequacy of the system as stemming from fundamentally negative attitudes to benefits and those who claim them:

Disabled people – and everybody on benefits – should be able to live a life and not have to struggle financially.
GROUP OF DISABLED PEOPLE, COVENTRY

We need to go back to the 1950s and the Bevan Report and see the system as a safety net and make sure no-one slips beneath it. You have to stop people using the system being seen as a scroungers' network, we need rights not privileges.

We need a basic belief that people have a right to benefits, and that the things that we get are enabling, not disabling.

We need to change society's attitude. We're forced to see people who are not working as scroungers and it just is not true, there are just not jobs there for people to go and get.
GROUP OF UNEMPLOYED WOMEN, GLOUCESTERSHIRE

I would like to see benefits rise to a decent level at which people can live reasonably rather than struggling on unrealistic budgets.
WOMAN, YORKSHIRE (35)

Young people stressed the need for more equality in the system:

Everybody should get the same amount of money regardless of age.
GROUP OF YOUNG PEOPLE FROM UK

Older people and others had clear and straightforward views on what needs to happen to pensions:

They've got to bring it up to more than it is at the moment.
GROUP OF CARERS, YORKSHIRE (D)

The welfare state should keep people secure in old age, and there should be more for disabled people.
GROUP OF ASIAN DISABLED PEOPLE, LONDON

We should all be tret same – equal pensions all the way round.
GROUP OF OLDER PEOPLE, YORKSHIRE

The basic pension should be sufficient for everybody to live in comfort. I don't say in luxury, but I do say in comfort.
GROUP OF OLDER PEOPLE, WOKING

One pensioner is freezing while another is roasting, that's just the way it is at the moment. We should all get a pension that we can live on, then we wouldn't need to mess about with these extra payments.
GROUP OF OLDER PEOPLE, YORKSHIRE

There was also a call for a more universal approach to the Cold Weather Allowance:

Everyone should be entitled to a heating allowance if they are on low incomes: it isn't only the old and young people who freeze to death.
LONE PARENT, YORKSHIRE (36)

The call for better support for carers received support from one disabled person who had a clear view on how this should be worked out:

If people care for their partner they should be paid the equivalent of somebody doing it as a job.
GROUP OF DISABLED PEOPLE, COVENTRY

One group thought through the problems that might arise if benefits were made too high:

If you're giving people a reasonable standard of living through benefits that takes away the need to work.

Yes, but they will have the need to work for luxuries.
GROUP OF PEOPLE ON LOW INCOME, WALES

The point made by the second speaker emphasises the overwhelming desire expressed by most welfare state service users who contributed to the Commission to obtain employment wherever it was possible and practical.

On the issue of crime and benefits, the same group identified a clear and commonsense way of breaking the link:

If every person has enough money to live on, it would be more cost-effective and would stop people going into crime. Nobody wants to be looking over their shoulder all the time to see if the gas or electric is going to catch them, or whether there's a TV detector van coming.
GROUP OF PEOPLE ON LOW INCOME, WALES

Other ideas for the future

Welfare state service users also had practical ideas to offer to improve the day-to-day working of the current system. For example, one former drug user suggested that benefits could be paid into a special bank where people could get advice on budgeting and draw money as they needed it rather than have it 'dwindle away in their pocket'.

Another innovative idea came from the group of people on low income in Wales. They run a community centre with a range of facilities for local people. They represent tenants' interests on various committees and run a low-interest loan scheme. It is run by people from the estate with personal experience of the problems experienced by residents. They said:

In some ways we are the experts because we live on the benefits ... I think that a more locally based office would make the system more responsive.

As well as improving the quality of life for people actually receiving benefits and pensions, raising the level and quality of support would also have a knock-on effect and bring improvements to the local economy and to other groups and budgets:

The rate of benefits should be raised to allow people a decent standard of living. If we had more money there would be more money to spend in the shops so it would help all round.
LONE PARENT, YORKSHIRE (37)

A substantial increase in the basic pension would be offset by savings in other benefits like housing benefit. It would make people feel more independent as they wouldn't have to keep asking for this and that to complement their sparse income.
GROUP OF OLDER PEOPLE, WOKING

2. The benefits trap

The benefits trap has been well documented and is widely recognised by both government and experts. It works in two ways: by making people financially worse off if they take low paid jobs and by making it difficult for them to undertake education and training while receiving benefits.

Second only to the immediate problems of getting by on very low incomes, the benefits trap was one of the *biggest* concerns for many of the people who gave evidence to the Commission. People's basic willingness – and desire – to find paid work is documented later in this Report in the section on the importance of employment. Their comments about the benefits trap need to be considered in this context. Participants had much to say about both the financial and training trap. We will look at each in turn.

The financial trap

The benefits system traps people financially by giving them a higher level of income and support than they would be able to obtain in many low paid jobs. Even where a person can obtain a wage at a similar level to their benefit, the loss of associated benefits, such as Housing Benefit, Council Tax Benefit, free prescriptions and dental care, makes it impossible for them to take up a job without becoming worse off financially. Parents are particularly vulnerable to becoming caught in the trap. For instance:

We don't want to live on benefits, we want to be able to go and get jobs and earn a decent wage. We want money to be spent on building up offices and other facilities so we can go out to work. Most people on social security want to go out and work. I know I do, but we want to be able to know that we're going to be better off for working. Obviously if you're going to be worse off there'll be no point going to work.
AFRO-CARIBBEAN GROUP, MIDLANDS

I could support myself apart from paying rent, but they said you're not entitled to other benefits so you're not entitled to Housing Benefit, so I had to give up work.
GROUP OF LONE PARENTS, WALES

I'm working now but I'm hardly any better off than when I was on benefit.
LESBIAN MOTHERS GROUP, GLASGOW

We'd love to earn £12,000 a year but we're stuck in a rut where we can only get jobs paying £2.50 – £4.00 an hour, so you're making more on benefits because of things like Housing Benefit and Council Tax Benefit.
AFRO-CARIBBEAN GROUP, MIDLANDS

You can earn about £15 a week on top of your benefits, then they start to take your money. It's not a lot, you should be allowed more.
GROUP OF PEOPLE WITH LEARNING DIFFICULTIES, LONDON

It's a vicious circle and you're going round and round ... You can survive on welfare, but it falls through when you try and break away

and better yourself, and you just haven't got a hope in hell. The moment you start to try and sort yourself out and get somewhere is the moment that you start to get penalised and you just end up back in the situation you were trying to get out of.
GROUP OF YOUNG PEOPLE FROM UK

The benefits system is actually stopping you working. I've just graduated so I should be able to get a good job, but I can't afford to start working.
GROUP OF LONE PARENTS, WALES

If you want to go out and get a job you're talking about earning over £200 a week to keep a house and your kids ... It's Catch 22 the way it is.
GROUP OF LONE PARENTS, GLASGOW

One response from government to resolve this problem was the introduction of Family Credit, a benefit designed to top-up the wages of people with children who are in low-paid employment. However, the people who gave evidence to the Commission clearly saw the help available through Family Credit as very limited. Some believed they would still be worse off taking a low paid job, and those in work found that they were little or no better off when working and claiming Family Credit:

It's the minimum. It's OK if you have a council house, but if you have a mortgage they won't give you anything towards it. There's no consistency there.
LESBIAN MOTHERS GROUP, GLASGOW

I claim Family Credit, I'm lucky I've got a job. But I sat down the other day and thought 'well, I would probably be better off claiming Income Support, but then I would just be a statistic.' But if I was on Income Support I wouldn't have to pay for Council Tax, I wouldn't have to pay for school dinners etc, but at the moment I have to pay it all from my wages and Family Credit.
GROUP OF PEOPLE ON LOW INCOME, WALES

This Credit nonsense they've dreamed up turns out to be an absolute waste of time when you look at it thoroughly.
LESBIAN MOTHERS GROUP, GLASGOW

So far political and media discussion about the 'benefits trap' has mainly been framed in terms of the over-generousness of benefits rather than the meanness of pay levels. The poor law principle that people in receipt of benefits should be worse off than those in the lowest paid work still exerts a powerful influence. The welfare state service users we spoke with offered an important corrective to this. Their starting point was the poverty of wage levels. They saw the lack of a minimum wage as contributing to the problem and as playing a central part in making it more difficult for people to come off benefits and take up jobs. For example:

It's everything being done on a low wage, because there's no minimum wage … so I've gone out to work and been worse off.
GROUP OF PEOPLE ON LOW INCOME, WALES

I got so sick and tired of the unemployment office pestering me about getting a job I ended up taking one that paid the grand wage of £105 for a seven day working week. How could I be expected to keep my family and home going on that? I need around £130.00 a week just to cover essentials, so I gave up the job and had to get by on reduced benefit for 26 weeks.
GROUP OF PEOPLE RECEIVING BENEFITS, YORKSHIRE

In the past people would moonlight and get ripped off. Today you're legally employed and you're ripped off.
GROUP OF PEOPLE ON LOW INCOME, WALES

Accessible child care

Another key issue for parents trying to get back to work was finding and paying for child care. This was particularly important for lone parents. This need has long been identified, but a massive gap continues to exist:

The system doesn't encourage one-parent families to go back to work. As a mother with a two-year-old daughter the cost of child care makes it impossible for me to go back to work. With Family Credit I worked out that I would be about £30 a week better off going to work full-time, but after the cost of child care I would only have about £10 more than I get now. They should look at having more child care places because there's nothing you can do at the moment.
GROUP OF LONE PARENTS, YORKSHIRE

After school care costs you about £12.50 a week for each child, which is a lot of money for a single parent, yet you cannot get work if you're stuck with paying child care.

GROUP OF LONE PARENTS, GLASGOW

What I would really like is child care ... they only allow me a small amount at the moment and I can't afford to pay for more.

Even if we can get a job and earn some money it's risky. If you need time off for any reason, like if your child is ill, and you haven't got a sympathetic boss, you have no choice but to give up work. Then you get penalised – you go back to the Social and tell them you were sacked and they say, 'Well I'm sorry, you gave up your job voluntarily to look after your child, so you have to wait before you can get full benefit.' The time's getting longer and longer, it's ridiculous. You've also got all the waiting for the benefits to come through anyway.

GROUP OF LONE PARENTS, WALES

Sickness, disability and the inflexibility of the system

Going from benefits to work is also difficult for people who have been receiving long term sickness and disability benefits. One person identified particular inflexibility in the system for chronically sick people:

People with chronic illness don't stand a chance because it is too inflexible to allow people to work for a limited time each week as their health permits.

ELDERLY WOMAN, LONDON (57)

The training trap

Most of the people who took part in the discussions organised by the Commission made it clear that they were very keen to improve their circumstances and their chances for employment through education and training. They saw these as a key route to changing their situation.

However, almost all the people who were receiving benefits had experienced difficulty with them as a result of taking or wanting to do a course or other form of training or education. Some had had to give up opportunities for training or education; others were forced to do courses on a part-time basis:

They make it so difficult to higher your educational standard and to help you support yourself, you're just stuck in a trap.

GROUP OF EX-DRUG USER PARENTS, SHEFFIELD

The benefits system is too inflexible for you to get an education. I'm doing a course that will take me a year-and-a-half to complete because I cannot do more than 16 hours a week without losing my benefits. I could finish the course in six months and then get a job and be out of the benefits system and saving them a shit load of money. I'm going to get a job as soon as I've finished college, and I don't see why I should struggle for so long just because the benefits system is so inflexible.
GROUP OF YOUNG PEOPLE FROM UK

They've taken everything away that would help you get back into work.
GROUP OF UNEMPLOYED WOMEN, GLOUCESTERSHIRE

I can go to college on a part-time basis, but if I try and do it full-time they reduce your benefit, so at the end of the day it will take me longer to get any sort of qualification because of the way they set it up. We couldn't live on a grant if I went to college full-time. You're just not supported in trying to achieve anything.
GROUP OF EX-DRUG USERS, SHEFFIELD

Accessible and affordable child care is as important for parents to take up training and educational opportunities as it is for them to go into employment, but it is in equally short supply:

It's impossible to go to college if you need child care. We can't afford nurseries.
GROUP OF TEENAGE MOTHERS, LINCOLNSHIRE

THE BENEFITS TRAP: THE FUTURE

Tackling the benefits trap continues to be an important challenge for the welfare state. Traditional arrangement have clearly failed people receiving benefits. The massive social security reforms from the 1980s onwards have failed to address this problem and indeed have made it worse for many people because of the additional restrictions imposed, for example to qualify as 'available for work' or 'actively job seeking'. Trapping people in the system has not only done them a cruel disservice; it has also clearly failed society in general.

The welfare state service users who contributed evidence to the Commission had clear proposals to offer to tackle the immediate problem of the benefits trap. Many of them point to the need for a major shift in government strategy.

Recent government policy has mainly addressed the issue by subsidising *employers*, for example, through Family Credit to top up low wages or the Job Seekers Allowance, pushing people into low paid employment. People who offered evidence to the Commission shifted the emphasis to supporting *individual citizens* in a variety of ways; both through the benefits system and the labour market, for example, by raising benefit levels, ensuring flexibility in benefits which would enable claimants to undertake training and education, by increasing the availability of child care and by improving wage levels. For example:

> *I think they should give incentives for single parents to go out to work. We should get a decent wage or a decent top-up so that it benefits us to go to out work.*
> LESBIAN MOTHERS GROUP, GLASGOW

> *They should still pay your rent and other things while you're on Family Credit.*
> GROUP OF TEENAGE MOTHERS, EDINBURGH

Some participants saw the introduction of a minimum wage as an essential step towards ending the benefits trap:

> *We need a minimum wage, good training and respect for individuals.*
> GROUP OF UNEMPLOYED WOMEN, GLOUCESTERSHIRE

> *If employers had to pay a minimum wage it would be above the benefits level and people would want to get jobs.*
> GROUP OF YOUNG PEOPLE FROM UK

The evidence which the Commission received strongly suggests that many people are being prevented from taking up employment because of low wages, and those who do take low paid work remain dependent on the support of the welfare state.

Even if the argument of some commentators that a minimum wage would reduce the overall number of jobs is accepted, and there isn't agreement about this, the evidence which we received from welfare state service users suggests that it would still offer the important gain of enabling people to come off benefits completely and take up the jobs which are available.

In addition to wage levels and top-up benefits, some participants felt that greater variety in the types of employment and the ways in which people are employed would make it easier for them to go out to paid work. For example:

There should be more jobs working from home with a decent wage, that would solve the problem of child care.
LONE PARENT, YORKSHIRE (36)

Participants also offered a new, more positive interpretation of 'workfare'. Members of one group suggested that the rules around claiming could be changed to allow people to work and earn some money while receiving benefits and that this would both give them more money and help people to remain motivated to work:

People are willing to go out and earn a bit extra, but you can't do that, so that makes people feel 'Why bother' and they sit back and accept it, it's not worth going out and doing something then having your money stopped.
GROUP OF UNEMPLOYED WOMEN, GLOUCESTERSHIRE

Two simple yet achievable ideas were offered to solve the child care problems which parents face when they go back into employment:

Child care should be paid for during the first year if you come off benefits. That would give you time to get into work and build up your skills.
GROUP OF LONE PARENTS, WALES

If schools could stay open after 3.30 pm till around 5.30 or 6 o'clock, and they could charge for looking after the kids during this time it would help us go out to work and raise some money for the schools.
GROUP OF LONE PARENTS, YORKSHIRE

Participants also suggested that the benefits system should help people gain new skills and knowledge.They offered simple solutions to restrictions on their access to training and education while claiming benefits:

You should be able to claim when you are a student or doing training. If you can't do this how can you get into work?
GROUP OF UNEMPLOYED WOMEN, GLOUCESTERSHIRE

The benefits system needs to be flexible so you can get an education.
GROUP OF YOUNG PEOPLE FROM UK

3. The administration of benefits

Conventional discussions of the benefits system tend not to focus on the detail of its operation. Politicians and conventional experts are generally more interested in the principles at work and the broad sweep of policy. Welfare state service users, on the other hand, know first hand how important the nature of its actual day-to-day functioning is. Frequently this has more impact on the purposes it actually serves and how it is used and experienced, than broader philosophies and values which are meant to underpin it. Participants in the Commission had much to say about how the benefits system works in practice. As we might expect, this is an issue of major significance for them.

I think also benefits and pensions are important, but I think the way they are handled, a person is handled, is very important ... how it is delivered.
ASIAN SUPPORT GROUP, LINCOLNSHIRE

Some people reported relatively good experiences of obtaining benefits:

I think I know my way around that part of the system well enough to know what I need to know.
LESBIAN MOTHERS GROUP, GLASGOW

My (benefits) office has been exceptional.
GROUP OF LONE PARENTS, WALES

Sometimes the DSS people can be quite helpful.
UNEMPLOYED DISABLED WOMAN, KENT (60)

However, this was a minority view. Most of the people who spoke to the Commission reported extremely negative experiences of applying for benefits. Their criticisms related to two main areas: the inefficiency of the system and the negative way in which it treated them. Complaints extended from practical difficulties, such as unnecessarily complicated forms, through to feelings of humiliation arising from the process of application and from the way they were dealt with by staff at benefits offices. Sometimes the two failings seemed to be inter-connected.

The general picture people presented of applying for benefits was that it was very unpleasant. For example:

> *You're just another body and you've got to be processed as quickly as possible.*
> GROUP OF DISABLED PEOPLE, COVENTRY

> *Claiming Income Support has been a nightmare with a capital 'N'. I started off in one office and they'd say fill out form A1, then B1, like they didn't know which one to give me. I fill it out and take it down there and they say 'OK, your claim's coming through.' A month later nothing's happened and they say, 'sorry it wasn't passed on to the right office'. So they send me to another office, and then another and it still hasn't been sorted out. They say it will definitely be sorted out today. It took about four months in the end. It's just a nightmare. And the people are just so rude to you, they just try to shift you off to someone else all the time, any way that they can.*
> GROUP OF YOUNG HOMELESS PEOPLE, LONDON

> *They make you feel dim and they make you feel degraded. You ask them a question and they make you feel as though you are thick. You ask them something but they won't explain it.*
> GROUP OF UNEMPLOYED PEOPLE, GLOUCESTERSHIRE

> *Why don't the Benefits Agency believe what applicants' own doctors/GPs tell them about their ill health/disability?*
> WOMAN PENSIONER, LONDON (57)

> *They seem to make it as difficult as possible for you to apply – like you don't get an envelope to send things back – and little things like that make me wonder if somebody's got a job to think up ways to make it more difficult to apply.*
> GROUP OF UNEMPLOYED PEOPLE, GLOUCESTERSHIRE

> *The Benefits Agency seems to treat everyone like idle scroungers when these are, in fact, a small minority.*
> WOMAN, KENT (25)

> *You can be there for hours filling forms in and you can't get any money.*
> GROUP OF TEENAGE MOTHERS, LINCOLNSHIRE

Communications with claimants needs improvement. There seems to be an attitude problem with some staff, they make you feel as if you are begging.
ELDERLY MAN, MANCHESTER (21)

One woman who completed a Commission questionnaire thought that the Citizen's Charter scheme had improved efficiency in handling claims, but she went on to say:

It's very difficult to get through the obstacle course of applying for benefits. One gets the feeling more and more that tho DSS arc trying to save money rather than do their job properly.
UNEMPLOYED DISABLED WOMAN, KENT (60)

A number of participants criticised the length and complexity of many of the forms used by the Benefits Agency. Some saw them as having been deliberately designed to catch people out. This is what members of one group said in their discussion:

The forms used to be a lot easier.

The Incapacity Benefit form I filled in was 12 pages.

You should try the Family Credit one.

Yes, you need a degree to do it.
GROUP OF PEOPLE ON LOW INCOME, WALES

This view was echoed in other evidence. For example:

The form is like a book. They ask you the same question five, six, seven, eight, even nine times. They do it to see if you repeat yourself or put different things down. That's the way the system works. The forms are so complicated that half the people don't understand them, and they're written like that specifically for that reason, and that's why so many people don't get the benefits they're entitled to. You need a good social worker to tell you how to do it, and that's unfair. I lost years of benefit because I never understood the forms.
AFRO-CARIBBEAN GROUP, MIDLANDS

The form for free prescriptions, eye and dental care is crap. The forms are off-putting and you loose out if you don't know how to fill them in. This makes the welfare state inaccessible.
ANONYMOUS (38)

A number of participants expressed considerable concern about the time it took to process claims:

> *The time you wait for them to deal with your claim is a real serious issue. I know if you're awarded the claim it's backdated, but you might have to live for months – not days or weeks – we're talking about months – without the money. You can't go to the bank and have an overdraft. The bank manager would just laugh.*

> *The waiting is terrible. They send you these forms, you fill them in, you send them off, and you wait and wait. You've got no way of knowing if they've received the form, if they're acting on the form, or when you can expect to receive a reply.*
> GROUP OF PEOPLE ON LOW INCOME, WALES

There were differences of opinion about the causes of shortcomings with the Benefits Agency. Some participants saw the problems as individualised, others identified wider issues.This can be seen from this extract from a discussion among a group of unemployed women:

> *They don't see us as human beings when they're one side of the counter and we're the other side.*

> *The rigid rules brought in by the government push staff to be Nazi-ish.*

> *It's pointless having a go at local people when they have no choice about what they implement.*

> *But it encourages their attitude, makes them more 'you've got to do as I say or else', rather than treating you as someone who uses the service.*
> GROUP OF UNEMPLOYED WOMEN, GLOUCESTERSHIRE

Wherever the origins of the problem lie, whether it is with poor policy or poor quality and poorly trained staff, or with the two magnifying each other's shortcomings, the result is destructive to service users and contrary to the stated aims of the benefits system:

> *I recognise that the clerks we see over the counter are just doing what they're told and they might not necessarily like the system. If they were just sitting in a room here like us and it was totally off the record I bet they would be saying the same things as us. And lots of them are also crying out for training to understand the system.*
> GROUP OF LONE PARENTS, WALES

The people are the problem. The system is a bit slow and drags and asks too many questions, but the people that I have met are just so rude. They treat you like a yo-yo and send you around to all the different offices. You get fares but you get nothing to make up for all of the energy you are burning off walking backwards and forwards trying to sort things out. They just degrade you to the point where you feel you can't be bothered claiming.
GROUP OF YOUNG HOMELESS PEOPLE, LONDON

You end up in a big queue and if you haven't got everything right there or it's not in your notes, or anything like that, they just won't deal with you, or they fob you off to somebody else. Then they tell you that you could have phoned in, but in my experience that's just another way of fobbing you off as they like to keep you at a distance.
GROUP OF EX-DRUG USER PARENTS, SHEFFIELD

It differs from person to person and office to office. I went down to one Child Support Agency office when I had problems with my ex-husband and they really looked after me well. They put me in a private room, offered to sit with me so I wasn't by myself and said they would do everything they could to help. The next day I went back to the same office and was treated completely differently. It really depends so much on who you see.
GROUP OF LONE PARENTS, WALES

It's their attitude when you go to them to try to explain something or ask a question. It's just the way they look at you as if to say 'Oh, another one of these people'. You can tell from their expression they're not really concerned, and they just sit there. I think half the time they're just interested in going for a tea break and they're not really listening. Then, when things go wrong and you haven't got your money, they just make excuses and say 'We've lost your records', or 'It's in the post'. You can go down there and you sit for hours on end, but they're just not bothered.
GROUP OF PEOPLE RECEIVING BENEFITS, YORKSHIRE

Some participants also highlighted the lack of accessible information on benefits. For instance:

There's lots of money in the system that people don't know about, for some of us our pride is too big to apply.
GROUP OF OLDER WOMEN, LONDON

If you were in the position of not having dealt with social security before, I think you'd find it very difficult to get the information that you need to know to find out what is available. I think they try and keep very much to themselves what you should be getting ... The whole thing has become a cash thing and I think they're trying to save money all the time. It shows in the service you get. You end up banging your head against a brick wall trying to get information.
GROUP OF EX-DRUG USER PARENTS, SHEFFIELD

Members of minority ethnic groups we spoke to described the particular problems their communities faced because of the lack of accessible information and application forms:

The laws are made in such a way that they are so complicated, especially for ethnic minority people, that when we apply for benefits we are often rejected and many are not aware of how to make an appeal. Many do not understand the information given because it is in English.

Every year we hear or read about so much money that has not been claimed, and I'm quite sure that many in the Asian community do not claim ... efforts should be made to make people aware of their entitlements.
GROUP OF ASIAN DISABLED PEOPLE, LONDON

One participant told of how their difficulties with information had been overcome by using the Benefits Enquiry Line provided by the Benefits Agency, but this had now been shut down.

I found out all the information about what I was entitled to through the Benefits Enquiry Line. Doing that it meant I was able to explain the information to my local benefits office and that really helped to speed things up. But that has been closed down now, and I wonder how many people will be able to get this sort of information now. I found it very difficult then, it will be worse now, and without the right information, there you are, lost in the system.
GROUP OF PEOPLE LIVING WITH HIV/AIDS, MANCHESTER

Many participants experienced humiliation in the process of claiming and qualifying for benefits. One disabled person described a particularly bad experience he had had when applying for Incapacity Benefit:

An Incapacity Benefit board is the most degrading thing to go

through, especially if you suffer with nerves. It's not like explaining a broken arm and it's difficult to sit with a stranger and try to explain things.
GROUP OF PEOPLE LIVING ON LOW INCOME, WALES

Another member of the same group contrasted the information that was required from claimants and MPs' reactions to public concern about them disclosing their outside earnings:

They don't want us to know about their outside influences, directorships and whatever. They say that's nothing to do with us, but they want to know everything that we ever have, every penny that we earn, every penny that our kids earn in interest if they've got money in a bank account.

The problems which welfare state service users reported in their dealings with the Benefits Agency went far beyond the process of applying and qualifying for benefits. The system clearly also adds to the difficulties and demoralisation of people who are already likely to be having a difficult time. For instance:

(I've been in a situation) where they buggered up, and you know they've buggered up, and they know they've buggered up, and you're expecting something and you're right on the edge: you've got no nappies for the kids, you've got no milk and your milk tokens are tied up ... you don't want to but you have to bleed your heart to them and say 'Look, help' and they go away and decide ... and so you'll have to come back in the morning. Well, what do I do now? So you find yourself going off to the Samaritans and the Salvation Army and that makes you feel even worse because of those images of homelessness and down-and-outs, and they're all those images that just seem to be you. That pushes you further away and you seem to be falling even further.
GROUP OF EX-DRUG USER PARENTS, SHEFFIELD

ADMINISTRATION OF BENEFITS: THE FUTURE

In their proposals for the future, people giving evidence to the Commission addressed both the need for the system to work better and for it to treat people better. They identified access to information as a key issue to make it easier for people to apply for benefits and to ensure that they received what they were entitled to. For instance:

There should be more information about benefits provided to people in all walks of life. This could be done through the media and through workshops with access for disabled people, signers for deaf people, equipment for blind people, and interpreters for people whose first language is not English.
WOMAN, LONE PARENT, BRISTOL (17)

There should be more outlets where information is available ... otherwise you're just left in a big queue.
GROUP OF EX-DRUG USERS, SHEFFIELD

Everyone should be able to understand welfare and be informed about it.
GROUP OF ASIAN DISABLED PEOPLE, LONDON

The system must become more accessible and less of an obstacle course, so that claimants, especially sick and disabled people, do not have to wade through a daunting system of complex forms. For example, it might be a good idea to have someone to help people with forms rather than them having to go to CABs etc. I would like the DSS to give people the impression that they are there to help rather than try to exclude them from help.
UNEMPLOYED DISABLED WOMAN, KENT (60)

The best way that I can see to improve both benefits and services would be to change the system so that instead of people having to chase around asking for what they need, things should be provided automatically. So, if you come under a certain set of criteria you get offered things straightaway. There should be someone to help you to do this, an advocate, so you don't get stressed out and your case is made properly.
GROUP OF PEOPLE LIVING WITH HIV/AIDS, MANCHESTER

There should be more advice on what you are entitled to claim.
GROUP OF PEOPLE LIVING ON LOW INCOME, WALES

There needs to be someone in between (the claimant and the Benefits Agency's officials) – a buffer system ... counsellors who can give some support and advice rather just saying 'no, no, no, we can't do that, you're too late' etc. This would also help people gain more confidence and get other things sorted out.
GROUP OF EX-DRUG USERS, SHEFFIELD

They should do their job and not make it so difficult.
GROUP OF TEENAGE MOTHERS, EDINBURGH

Participants emphasised the need to challenge the negative stereotyping of claimants in the benefits system and the hostile way in which they were frequently treated. Many stressed that claimants should receive better treatment. For example, people who sign on as unemployed are now required to sign contracts to say that they are looking for work. One group suggested this should work both ways:

We now have to sign a contract to say we're looking for work and doing all these things so that we get our benefit, but as soon as they mess up we don't get any sort of apology. If it was us who let them down on their contract they would be down on you and your money would be stopped.

It should be like a joint contract. It's part of their job to keep you in a healthy state. If your money is three or four days late it upsets the family and the kids, but all you get is a letter saying, 'We're very sorry but so-and-so happened ...' They should be a lot more accountable for their problems and the problems they cause.When you've signed and made your commitment and things don't happen, that's very frustrating.
GROUP OF EX-DRUG USER PARENTS, SHEFFIELD

A key component which participants identified to reform the benefits system was improving the quality of the face to face relationships that people experienced within it. This demanded a new culture, at the heart of which would be a positive change in the way in which it treated people:

We want to have a good service, and the people who are running the service should be helpful and friendly towards the people who need it.
GROUP OF OLDER WOMEN, LONDON

They should be trained in how to treat people ... I honestly think respect is the main thing.
GROUP OF PEOPLE ON LOW INCOME, WALES

CHAPTER 5

Welfare state services: Present and future

While people giving evidence to the Commission had much to say about benefits, they also gave evidence about other welfare state services. This included the National Health Service, social services and community care, housing, transport, education and training and leisure. We begin with the National Health Service.

The National Health Service

Participants regarded the National Health Service as the second most important part of the welfare state after benefits and pensions. As with benefits, some people who were not actually using the service currently said that it was reassuring to know the NHS would be there if they did need it.

In the group discussions, welfare state service users spent much less time talking about the NHS than the benefits system. Evidence from individuals submitted on questionnaires was more balanced in the attention which it gave to the NHS and benefits. From the comments people did make, it does not seem likely that they were less concerned about the NHS than they were about benefits.

A more plausible explanation for the variation in the focus of their concerns is that inadequacies in the benefits system have a day-to-day and all-embracing effect on people's lives. For most people the health service is something which they are more likely to think about when they need it. Furthermore while evidence on the benefits system focussed on its many flaws, most of participants' concerns about the NHS were concerned with fears about it being run down, rather than its essential nature.

Issues of concern

People were very concerned about the effect of cuts which have already been made to the NHS and were also worried about whether it would be available in the future.

I would like all of us to get better help from the hospital.
GROUP OF OLDER WOMEN, LONDON

The hospitals are closing down and the cut backs are destroying the ones we still have, which makes no sense when the population's getting bigger, and we seem to have more diseases and cancers and problems from air pollution and one thing and another.
GROUP OF PEOPLE RECEIVING BENEFITS, YORKSHIRE

People are being refused treatments that are available for HIV/AIDS until they become ill, because of lack of money. What's happened to the Hippocratic oath and caring for people? I can go to hospital and sit in a nice furnished waiting room. It looks nice and it's comfortable, but I'm not there to look at the decor. I'm there to get treatment.

I come from France and I am used to the health service meaning free, universal and immediate access, which is not what happens in this country and I always find this shocking.
GROUP OF PEOPLE LIVING WITH HIV/AIDS, MANCHESTER

Money is going into administration instead of where it's really needed.
GROUP OF CARERS, YORKSHIRE (D)

They keep you waiting for hours.
GROUP OF PEOPLE WITH LEARNING DIFFICULTIES, LONDON

Like with the National Health now they're turning people away from important operations and you're waiting an age for an appointment that you really, really need.

They're closing hospitals for no reason at all, yet there's not enough beds. I had a situation when my brother had cancer, my sister, who's also elderly and ill, had to look after him until they got him into hospital. We did get help from a district nurse eventually, but why should the onus fall on people like me in my position?
GROUP OF DISABLED PEOPLE, YORKSHIRE

Our hospital has become a centre of excellence for treating people with HIV and they come from other areas for treatment here, but they are now having trouble with getting their health authorities to pay for the treatment there. Now even people who live here are being denied access to the treatment that they need. Things have become very hit

*and miss and what's available to some people isn't there for
others.*
GROUP OF PEOPLE LIVING WITH HIV/AIDS, MANCHESTER

*You don't get support in the hospital either because as soon as you
start to get a bit better, then you're out of the door.*
GROUP OF DISABLED PEOPLE, COVENTRY

We've lost the universality of the NHS.
GROUP OF OLDER PEOPLE, WOKING

As in other policy areas, people from ethnic minorities experienced
discrimination when using health services:

*Asian people are not assessed properly and they are sent home
after an operation and it is assumed that their family will take care of
them, but they do not make sure of this and it is not always so.*
GROUP OF ASIAN DISABLED PEOPLE, LONDON

Many of the current problems were seen as the result of reforms to
the NHS, and most people believe the changes that have taken
place have been a poor use of resources and taken money out of
care and increased management and administration unnecessarily:

*There has been tremendous waste on the reorganisation of the
health service and getting managers to run the system rather than
doctors and nurses. There has been a tremendous increase in
bureaucracy, and let's face it, it's all been jobs for the boys.*

There's an emphasis on money instead of patients.
GROUP OF OLDER PEOPLE, WOKING

*Resources in the health services are not well used. Too much is
spent on administration and not enough on treatment. There are too
many quangos and too many people wanting authority and power.*
GROUP OF PEOPLE LIVING WITH HIV/AIDS, MANCHESTER

Others pointed to day-to-day inefficiency:

*I arrived for an out-patients appointment and they'd lost my file. It
took a nurse half an hour to track it down, and this happened with at
least two other people while I was waiting. Then someone came in
for an appointment that had been made by a ward while they were
an in-patient, but the ward hadn't told the clinic; and one poor
woman was brought in by hospital transport on the wrong day. This*

was in the space of a couple of hours at one clinic at one hospital.
ANONYMOUS (24)

NHS: THE FUTURE

Participants were still committed to the founding principles of the National Health Service, services which were universally available and free at the point of use:

Health services must remain available to all irrespective of income.
ELDERLY WOMAN, SURREY (61)

We need a health service that meets the needs of the community with less bureaucracy.
ANONYMOUS (24)

All health services should be free, including dentists and opticians.
GROUP OF LONE PARENTS, WALES

To be in a caring society with the NHS, in fact even if it means paying more.
WOMAN, LONDON (16)

More money's needed to put into hospitals. There's more money needed to go into nursing homes and more nursing homes need to be built.
GROUP OF DISABLED PEOPLE, YORKSHIRE

People also had positive suggestions to make about how pressure on the NHS could be relieved and it could be a 'health' rather than an 'illness' service. For example:

There should be more preventative activities and services for elderly people so that you don't use the Health Service so much and we keep ourselves healthy and active.
GROUP OF OLDER WOMEN, LONDON

Another suggestion was that people should value the service more, and that there could be safeguards to encourage this, like some form of penalty on those who failed to keep appointments.

Community care and social services

Community care and social services have become an increasingly important part of the welfare state. In many areas, social services make up the largest single local authority budget. Growing proportions and numbers of old and particularly very old people and moves towards providing support in people's homes rather than removing them to institutions, have placed increasing significance on these services. Community care includes a range of needs and issues which have become increasingly important on both political and public agendas, including long term care, disability and 'mental health'. Community care policy in the UK has undergone major reform and further changes are likely in social services. The direction of policy has been away from statutory provision to the purchase of services from non-statutory agencies, with an increased emphasis on 'economy' and 'cost-effectiveness'.

In their evidence, participants raised a wide range of issues about social and community care services. Concerns were expressed by a wide range of groups and individuals, notably by carers, disabled and older people, mental health service users and lone parents. Crucial areas of concern were increasing restrictions on access to such services, their variable, often poor, quality and unsuitability.

The level of participants' concerns about community care was very high. Many expressed fundamental fears and anxieties:

I'm very worried about community care in old age. Once upon a time we thought that we were going to have free care for the rest of our lives, but now it seems that we're going to have to pay for this sort of care.
GROUP OF OLDER WOMEN, LONDON

When you (mental health service users) leave hospital you should have a community care nurse or a social worker, but you just get chucked out with nothing.
GROUP OF DISABLED PEOPLE, COVENTRY

Care in the community was falling down from the beginning.
GROUP OF CARERS, YORKSHIRE (D)

Patients are being discharged without proper assessments under the Community Care Act and people pass away before they get proper services.
GROUP OF ASIAN DISABLED PEOPLE, LONDON

I was told that I would get less support from social services because

I live with my carer. I was told that they would make sure I had a phone to use in case of emergency, but they said because my partner was with me, he could go to the phone box over the road. But what happens if he's having a night off or goes out?
GROUP OF PEOPLE LIVING WITH HIV/AIDS, MANCHESTER

I've never had a full assessment – and I used to be a social worker!
GROUP OF DISABLED PEOPLE, COVENTRY

I was told there was no way I could get someone to sit with my severely disabled son one night a week while I did a course. Then, when I said that I was thinking of having him put into full-time care, arrangements miraculously became possible.
GROUP OF LONE PARENTS, WALES

While service users and carers had been encouraged to believe that the community care reforms would result in more and better services, the strong message from the evidence received by the Commission was that levels of services and support were inadequate and being reduced all over the country. For example:

I think we're often begging for services because there isn't enough to go around. The services are there, but they're spread over such a big field. Look at day centres and day respite in our area. We've got about seven centres in Leeds, how many carers can that help? So the problem isn't that services aren't there, it's that you're one of a thousand people going for 150 places.
GROUP OF CARERS, YORKSHIRE (A)

There's so many cut backs in social services that they're not helping the people that need them.
AFRO-CARIBBEAN GROUP, MIDLANDS

They're cutting a lot of our coaches for the day centre.
GROUP OF PEOPLE WITH LEARNING DIFFICULTIES, LONDON

There is an impression that all Asian people are rich and do not need services and support, but not all Asian people are rich.
GROUP OF ASIAN DISABLED PEOPLE, LONDON

Home helps services and the like are almost non-existent.
GROUP OF OLDER PEOPLE, WOKING

I know the social services are there, but they're very pushed and you

feel that unless it's an emergency you don't want to bother them.
GROUP OF CARERS, YORKSHIRE (D)

People in rural areas felt particularly neglected by services:

There is just no provision and it's difficult to access (services), for most things you have to travel 20 miles to the city, which is difficult if you are on a low income.
GROUP OF UNEMPLOYED WOMEN, GLOUCESTERSHIRE

The welfare state service users we spoke with saw a need for flexibility in services:

I might be happy with the service I get, but that doesn't mean to say that my next door neighbour in the same circumstances is as happy as I am.
GROUP OF CARERS, YORKSHIRE (B)

One woman who took part in a group discussion gave an example of how resources were wasted, and people's lives impoverished, because of inflexibility in the community care system:

My mother's 82 and the DSS are paying £352 a week to keep my mother in a nursing home. She doesn't want to be there and she doesn't need 24 hour care, she just needs to have somebody around. I can't do this all the time, I've got two children and one of them needs a lot of attention. I could give her most of the care she needs at home with a little support that would cost a lot less, but they won't pay it. It's criminal.
GROUP OF LONE PARENTS, WALES

There was considerable adverse criticism of community care practice and the way in which services were actually provided:

They send me carers from an agency to help look after my 92 year old uncle, but I usually help them as they're not trained and usually do not want to work.
WOMAN CARER, SURREY (58)

There's a big variation in quality of service from place to place. My wife's been coming to the Green Centre and it's been marvellous. But when she went to another place nobody wanted to do anything for her and she sat there all day.
GROUP OF CARERS, YORKSHIRE (A)

You come up against the people who are providing the services who have ageist views and/or are not keen on people from other countries, and that makes life very difficult.
GROUP OF OLDER WOMEN, LONDON

They rush us at the day centre. They assume that they know what you want.
GROUP OF PEOPLE WITH LEARNING DIFFICULTIES, LONDON

They insist on everything being black and white to fit users into their categories.
ELDERLY WOMAN, LONDON (57)

They tend to make us feel we're begging for something.
GROUP OF OLDER WOMEN, LONDON

They always try to tell you what you want. It should be the other way round.
GROUP OF DISABLED PEOPLE, COVENTRY

While the system of support is now called *community* care, many people are still being placed in residential institutions. Participants with experience of such settings were critical of their quality:

You're just thrown into a place and that's it. The majority (of people in homes) are just sat around watching television or looking out of the window.
GROUP OF CARERS, YORKSHIRE (D)

There has been considerable controversy and debate about the issue of older people having to contribute towards the cost of residential care and particularly about them having to sell their homes to do so. Older people who took part in the Commission expressed extreme unhappiness at this situation:

It's very unfair that someone's got to sell their home to pay for residential care, when someone has spent all their life working to buy their house and they want to leave it for their children. Then somebody who hasn't been thrifty can go into care and they are paid for.
GROUP OF OLDER PEOPLE, WOKING

When my wife started being poorly, I talked it over with my daughter and I sold our bungalow and I gave the money to her. Now, if I hadn't

*done that I would probably have had to sell the bungalow and give
the money to the state for my wife's residential care.*
GROUP OF CARERS, YORKSHIRE (A)

*I want to be able to live in my own home and not have to sell my
house to pay for services in a residential home.*
ELDERLY MAN, MIDDLESEX (23)

Residential services are not the only community care provision for
which people are now being required to pay. As a result of
government policy, local authorities are increasingly making service
users pay fees for services like home care and bath nurses. There is
no uniformity in how these fees are determined or assessed and
they have generally risen since their introduction. Welfare state
service users who spoke to the Commission saw such charges as a
penalty being imposed on service users:

*Whatever you need, they should not take your money situation into
it.*
GROUP OF CARERS, YORKSHIRE (B)

*The council is imposing charges for home care. Surely welfare
should be free.*
GROUP OF ASIAN DISABLED PEOPLE, LONDON

Some of us have to pay, but others don't.
GROUP OF PEOPLE WITH LEARNING DIFFICULTIES, LONDON

*You pay for service, and quite highly: £16 a week for a home help
and £8 for a bath nurse. If you can't pay, you go without.*
GROUP OF OLDER PEOPLE, WOKING

COMMUNITY CARE: THE FUTURE

Participants' ideas for how community care could be improved,
suggested that the community care reforms did not so much offer a
new and better way forward, as represent an unhelpful diversion.
Reliability and *quality* were welfare state service users' own priorities
for the future:

*We should go back to a regime of providing all services in the best
possible manner, not working out what kind of services can be
provide within the limits of budgets.*
GROUP OF ASIAN DISABLED PEOPLE, LONDON

We would feel better about using services if the services were better quality.
GROUP OF PEOPLE WITH LEARNING DIFFICULTIES, LONDON

It's not so much the quality of the service, it's the security of knowing that needs are taken into account as they arise and not be left wondering whether there will be a service.
GROUP OF ASIAN DISABLED PEOPLE, LONDON

Welfare state service users highlighted two new priorities. The first of these was for people to have more control over the services and support which they received and the second was for these to be more imaginative and flexible in design and operation.

There was widespread support for improving services by ensuring that users of community care had increased choice and control over how they are provided:

(Agencies and services should) find out what service users need, what people need, and consult people who are going to use the service, to get the users to say what they want from the service.
GROUP OF OLDER WOMEN, LONDON

People should always be given choice in relation to services, and they should provide culturally sensitive services.
GROUP OF ASIAN DISABLED PEOPLE, LONDON

We should have more of a say in services and be more involved.
GROUP OF PEOPLE WITH LEARNING DIFFICULTIES, LONDON

A lot of work needs to be done in order to see whether the welfare that is being provided is that which is needed.
GROUP OF ASIAN DISABLED PEOPLE, LONDON

More flexible and innovative services which were responsive to people's needs were envisaged as part and parcel of such increased user control. Participants saw a strong need for services to develop in this way:

Services should be flexible, providing help when it is needed for people with fluctuating conditions.
ELDERLY WOMAN, LONDON (57)

I'd like to see something between hospitals and nursing homes where

*a person with dementia who doesn't need medical help but needs
day-to-day help can get the support they really need.*
GROUP OF CARERS, YORKSHIRE (A)

*There should be less stereotyping of people, then there will be more
understanding of different needs of different sections of the
community. To do this we need more people from ethnic minority
communities in the workforce at service points.*
GROUP OF ASIAN DISABLED PEOPLE, LONDON

*I would like to have services that enable me to be independent and
empower me to do what I want to do. For example, as a blind
person I find it very difficult to do shopping on my own, so I need
someone to help me, but to do that at the moment I have to pay
somebody or ask a volunteer for help, and that can sometimes be
difficult. So I want services that will help me to be an independent
individual.*
GROUP OF DISABLED PEOPLE, COVENTRY

Putting resources into prevention rather than delaying until people's
physical or mental condition deteriorated was also seen as a way
both of ensuring appropriate support and ensuring real economy
and efficiency. For instance:

*More should be done before people get really frail. I think a lot of
people get support when they're really frail and can't look after
themselves. If we had more remedial services, such as home helps
and help with baths, it would keep people independent for longer.
That would be better because when people become desperate they
have to go into a home and that costs an awful lot. If more money
were spent on prevention, people wouldn't begin to feel they
couldn't cope.*
GROUP OF OLDER PEOPLE, WOKING

Participants emphasised the need for community care workers to
be skilled and capable and to treat service users positively and with
respect. For example:

*We want to have a good service, and the people who are running
the service should be helpful and friendly towards the people who
need it.*

Most of us older people have low expectations of what we should

*have and feel we don't deserve it ... People who give us the service
should show that they welcome us and that we're entitled to it.*
GROUP OF OLDER WOMEN, LONDON

People should do their jobs properly.
GROUP OF PEOPLE WITH LEARNING DIFFICULTIES, LONDON

Carers identified several modest and specific initiatives which would
improve their situation:

*We need a visitor for carers, to keep an eye on us, make sure that
we're coping, to see if we need a break.*

*There should be somewhere or a helpline for carers to get
information.*

*If we could have somebody coming in, even for just half a day, so we
can get out to the dentist, hairdressers, and all those personal things
you need to do. It doesn't need to be a long time, it just needs to be
regular and dependable.*
GROUP OF CARERS, YORKSHIRE (D)

One disabled person spoke for many more:

I want to be able to employ my own personal assistants.
DISABLED PERSON ON BENEFITS (29)

For this person and for others in the same situation and with the
same desire to be in control of the assistance that they receive, there
is some chance of their aim being realised. This is one small area of
the system which is changing in response to service users' views.
The practice of employing personal assistants with local authority
funding, instead of being offered a pre-set menu of services, is a
development which was pioneered by the disabled people's
movement and is currently enjoyed by a small number of disabled
people. With the passage of the Community Care (Direct Payments)
Act in 1996, there is now a genuine prospect of self-run support
independent living schemes becoming more generally available for
community care service users.

Housing

The issue of housing was only raised infrequently in the
Commission's discussions with welfare state service users. Even at

the session with a local residents group at a community centre, it did not come up for discussion without prompting.

While the provision of public housing was a central plank in the creation of the welfare state, many people taking part in the Commission did not seem to think of it in these terms. We don't know whether the sale of council housing or the ending of council house building are related to this, but certainly a sense of housing as part of the welfare state seems to have been diluted.

Where welfare state service users did discuss housing, they were very critical of current social housing provision. For many people it was out of reach: there just wasn't enough of it. For example:

I needed somewhere suitable for my four children. After three years on the waiting list I just gave up and had to rent privately and find the extra money from my benefits.
GROUP OF DISABLED PEOPLE, YORKSHIRE

We should have some personal choice in housing. That means that the government has to think about building more housing to meet people's needs.
GROUP OF OLDER PEOPLE, LONDON

We need more houses. It's an ordeal looking for houses.
GROUP OF PEOPLE WITH LEARNING DIFFICULTIES, LONDON

Now you can't get on the waiting list if they think your income is too high, even if it's not enough to afford anywhere for yourself.
MALE MENTAL HEALTH SERVICE USER RECEIVING BENEFITS, SHEFFIELD (28)

We have a lot of hidden homelessness in rural areas – people sleeping in the woods and on friend's floors, but it's not as visible as urban homelessness so nothing gets done about it.
GROUP OF UNEMPLOYED WOMEN, GLOUCESTERSHIRE

I'm 80 and have just had my council flat decorated. I told them I'm getting older now and can't afford it, but they say they will only decorate when people move in.
GROUP OF CARERS, YORKSHIRE (D)

What housing was available was often of poor quality or inappropriate:

Housing provision needs to be better suited to the needs of individuals. At the moment they do not really give options when you are offered housing. You get two offers of housing with the option to refuse the offer, and if you refuse them both, you lose your chance of being housed by the council. Yet it might be difficult or more expensive to live in a particular area. What's the point of forcing me to live in an area where it's going to be too expensive for me to get to my college?
GROUP OF YOUNG HOMELESS PEOPLE, LONDON

When houses are allocated they're often in poor condition, and you've no choice but to take it, and you're stuck in a slum with no money to redecorate.
GROUP OF PEOPLE ON LOW INCOME, WALES

You come out of drug rehabilitation and all they seem to give you is housing in the areas that we're trying to get away from and houses that are falling to bits ... Then they wonder why they've got a drug problem.
GROUP OF EX-DRUG USERS, SHEFFIELD

The lack of new council housing was highlighted by one local group:

It's dropped off drastically. If there were enough houses being built the points system would probably work.

We've just had some houses demolished, but there's not a lot being built to replace them.
GROUP OF PEOPLE ON LOW INCOME, WALES

Single homeless people also highlighted problems in the system of allocating council housing:

You go to the interview and they tell this and that about the type of place they're offering you, and when you get there it's nothing like you were told, but you have to take it because if you turn it down they end up saying you're not that desperate.

The council has all these criteria for housing. You have to be vulnerable, have a child or some sort of health problem before they will offer you a place. I asked to be rehoused because my home was overcrowded and they said I hadn't got a real reason to be rehoused and I would have to go to a hostel. That's just not fair, and it would just end up giving me the type of problems that would give them a reason to re-house me.
GROUP OF YOUNG HOMELESS PEOPLE, LONDON

The introduction of water meters in new housing association properties was identified as creating an additional set of problems for poor people:

> *People on Income Support are frightened to use water and the family shares a bath, so they're going to have health problems.*
> GROUP OF UNEMPLOYED WOMEN, GLOUCESTERSHIRE

Teenage mothers have been the focus of political and media attacks for council house 'queue jumping'. They have been condemned for getting pregnant to get rehoused. The reality they reported was very different:

> *You get nothing, just a lot of hassle ... You wait for ages and ages.*
> GROUP OF TEENAGE MOTHERS, EDINBURGH

> *I went to put my name down on the housing register and I got a letter straight back saying I wasn't eligible because I was only 16.*
> GROUP OF TEENAGE MOTHERS, LINCOLNSHIRE

HOUSING: THE FUTURE

The few people who did talk about housing emphasised the importance of improving both the the quality and suitability of social housing. While quantity is clearly important and currently insufficient, it is not enough. For example:

> *What needs to be done is to assess the needs of people in terms of social and cultural issues, particularly people with disabilities. Now if you start considering that, then you think in terms of the type of house, the location and facilities, and not just numbers of units.*
> GROUP OF ASIAN DISABLED PEOPLE, LONDON

> *When I say we need new houses I mean they need to be a lot more like homes. They should be building communities, not just a load of houses alongside the road.*
> GROUP OF PEOPLE ON LOW INCOME, WALES

Participants also highlighted the need for improvements in housing allocation policy, both to match housing with need and to ensure equal access:

> *If you are offered a house and it's not suitable or it's in the wrong*

*area you should be able to turn it down and ask for something else
without prejudicing your entitlement.*

*The councils must improve the system for housing allocation and
there needs to be more provision for single homeless people.*
GROUP OF YOUNG HOMELESS PEOPLE, LONDON

Housing was seen as playing an essential part in the welfare of the
population when the welfare state was created. More recently
emphasis has again been placed on it as a private responsibility and
commodity. Welfare state service users were still conscious of the
interrelation of different parts of the welfare state and the need for
them to work together. One person restated the crucial connection
between improving housing and improving health:

*Money needs to be put into improving housing. This would help ease
the burden on the NHS as bad housing conditions cause many
medical problems.*
LONE PARENT, YORKSHIRE (37)

Transport

While massive amounts of public money have been spent both on
public transport and the road system, very few participants saw
transport as part of the welfare state. Some of the groups we spoke
to saw public transport as part of the support provided by
government, when we prompted them, but most seemed to see this
as separate from the welfare state. None of the questionnaires which
we received from individuals mentioned the issue of transport.
    Disabled people had most to say on the subject and they were
scathing about their lack of access to 'public' transport:

*People with disabilities can't have choice, can't do anything without
reasonable transport, and it seems to be getting worse instead of better.*
GROUP OF OLDER WOMEN, LONDON

*Many disabled people have very little mobility due to the lack of
appropriate transport. There was a good scheme in London called
Taxicard (which provided subsidised taxi travel for disabled people
denied access to buses and trains), but they now have restrictions on
this, and you cannot make so many trips, so I have to look at my card
and see how many trips I have done and to economise.*
GROUP OF ASIAN DISABLED PEOPLE, LONDON

I pay my taxes towards a transport system that I can't access.
GROUP OF DISABLED PEOPLE, COVENTRY

People in rural areas had similar views:

If you live in a rural area you can't access transport.
GROUP OF UNEMPLOYED WOMEN, GLOUCESTERSHIRE

TRANSPORT: THE FUTURE

While public transport is clearly a key public policy issue, raising social, economic and environmental issues, it continues to be dogged by political and ideological arguments about whether it should be provided by state or the market. The comments made to the Commission suggest that the current public transport system is not meeting the needs of all citizens, and that these needs are not being met by the market. Disabled people who can afford to are forced into disproportionate car use because of the inaccessibility of 'public' transport. Other groups are denied access to transport, both public and private, by their low income.

The question remains whether all the needs which public transport is seen to address, including those of efficiency, ecology, social need and personal safety, can be met without large scale public investment and provision.

Education and training

While many participants did not expressly see education and training as part of the welfare state, most attached central importance to them, both as a means of improving their lives and opportunities and those of people close to them, particularly in relation to employment. One comment summed up a much broader view:

You can't get anything unless you've got education. Without education you can't get anywhere.
GROUP OF YOUNG PEOPLE FROM UK

I've put down education first, because without education you don't stand a chance of getting a good job.
ASIAN SUPPORT GROUP, LINCOLNSHIRE

*Most important for me is education and training to help me progress
in my career, help support my family*
YOUNG UNEMPLOYED MAN, BRISTOL (19)

A large proportion of the people who took part in group discussions
were taking educational and training courses, and many of them had
had to struggle with the benefits system to be allowed to do this. We
have discussed the difficulties they reported earlier in the section on
the benefits trap.

In addition to concerns about their own opportunities for
education and training, parents prioritised the education available to
their children.

Young people are our main concern because they're the future.
GROUP OF PEOPLE ON LOW INCOME, WALES

*I'd like to see a brighter future for my kiddies in terms of educating
themselves.*
GROUP OF EX-DRUG USER PARENTS, SHEFFIELD

Despite the value people put on education, they were disenchanted
with what the state system was offering their children:

We're not even getting basic education.
AFRO-CARIBBEAN GROUP, MIDLANDS

*If you've got a good catchment area you can get a bit of education,
but if you've got a bad area ...*
LESBIAN MOTHERS GROUP, GLASGOW

*Our children are not getting the opportunities and they're not going to
have the abilities because it's being knocked out of them. Our
children are going to form the 'underclass' for the next generation and
they are not going to get opportunities to progress. Two or three
generations down the line that gap is going to get wider and wider. I
think that's criminal because our kids have as much potential as
everybody else's. We're not asking for anything special or different,
we just want our children to be treated equally.*
GROUP OF LONE PARENTS, WALES

*If a kid's quite academic the teachers are fine, but if your kid's a bit
slow they don't seem to bother.*

Nurseries should come first for kids, it shouldn't matter if you've got

*money or not ... It's getting to the stage where they've not got
nurseries and a lot of kids are just going straight into school.*
GROUP OF LONE PARENTS, GLASGOW

*They've cut back so much in education that the people they're
paying to do the jobs aren't even able to carry out the function they
are being paid for, which isn't good use of resources.*
GROUP OF UNEMPLOYED WOMEN, GLOUCESTERSHIRE

The views of parents were reinforced by the experiences of some of
the younger people who gave evidence, who had left education
relatively recently:

You come out with no qualifications and you can't get a job.

*The education system has got so crap that people can't wait to get
out of it.*

*At the school that I went to, all the brainy ones did all right, the
teacher spent lots of time with them. But problem kids and the ones
that messed around like the rest of us didn't get so much attention. If
they spent more time with kids with problems maybe some of them
wouldn't end up on drugs. They just put it down to being idle, but it's
not.*
GROUP OF EX-DRUG USERS, SHEFFIELD

Some parents were critical of the hidden costs of sending children
to school. While state education is basically free, additional costs
like uniforms, books, writing equipment, sports kits, outings and
school dinners can be difficult for people on low incomes to meet:

*It's costing me more and more every year to send the kids to school,
for all the extras that used to be provided by the schools like trips
and outings.*

*School dinners now cost £1.05 a day, so they're costing me £11 a
week (for two children).*
GROUP OF PEOPLE ON LOW INCOME, WALES

The amount of fundraising carried out by schools was also a
problem for some parents:

*There's always a letter every week asking for money or sponsors. I
understand why they need it, but it's not the best way to do it,
sending children round knocking on strangers' doors.*

GROUP OF PEOPLE ON LOW INCOME, WALES

Education grants are available to help people on low incomes pay for school uniforms, but they were generally seen as inadequate:

You get clothing grants and it's like £50 and you can pay up to £40 for a pair of shoes. If your child grows out of his shoes you don't have £40 for another pair.

There's no way you can buy trousers, socks, jumpers, skirts, plus shoes for just £50. It's totally unrealistic.
LESBIAN MOTHERS GROUP, GLASGOW

Several parents talked about the importance of school meals for their children:

They're cutting back on school meals, but some kids don't get a warm meal at night, they depend on a decent meal at lunchtime.
LESBIAN MOTHERS GROUP, GLASGOW

Particular concerns were raised about education for disabled children and the need for appropriate support and facilities for them in mainstream education:

Facilities and services depend very much on the type of school, and it is very important that the needs of disabled people are not lost in the changes in the education system.

What usually happens nowadays for children with disabilities is that they are provided with whatever education is available, rather than meeting their real needs. This can mean that they are not ready for later life and independence.

There is a great tendency to send disabled children to specialist schools, but why not provide equipment and facilities at mainstream schools so they can mix with other children, who will then grow up knowing the needs of disabled people?
GROUP OF ASIAN DISABLED PEOPLE, LONDON

Education is not only for the young and many older people were concerned about the decreasing opportunities for and increasing cost of adult education classes:

I'd like to see education and leisure come to the fore, so that lots of us can take up the things we want.
GROUP OF OLDER WOMEN, LONDON

*A lot of us (older people) benefit from adult education. It's an
important part of our lives.*
GROUP OF OLDER PEOPLE, WOKING

People with learning difficulties who contributed evidence to the
Commission felt classes were becoming expensive:

It goes up every year.
GROUP OF PEOPLE WITH LEARNING DIFFICULTIES, LONDON

They also criticised a lack of suitable classes for them to attend.

Training

Successive governments have stressed their commitment to the
large scale creation of employment training schemes, both to help
unemployed people, particularly those who are long term
unemployed, return to work and to provide a start in employment
for young people. However, people with experience of such
schemes criticised them for not leading to employment:

*My son did an apprenticeship scheme with a plumbing firm and he
was bringing in money and doing all right. But at the end of two
years they had the choice to take him on or get another apprentice.
So they just kicked him out because they reckoned they couldn't
afford the wage, so they've just got another apprentice doing the
same work.*
GROUP OF PEOPLE ON LOW INCOME, WALES

*You want to have a job at the end of it ... but you go straight back on
the dole.*
GROUP OF YOUNG PEOPLE FROM UK

*What I can't understand is if there's enough work to be done to
create places on employment training, then why aren't there the
actual jobs to do this work? How come they just get people off the
dole to do training and give them £10 a week extra when there's
obviously a job there that needs doing for a full time worker?*
GROUP OF UNEMPLOYED PEOPLE, YORKSHIRE

EDUCATION AND TRAINING: THE FUTURE

Participants in the Commission found much wanting in both state
education and training. They wanted to see improvements in both.

While they did not identify specific measures which they would like to see, they stressed the need for change to ensure that they met both people's individual and collective rights and needs:

Education should be about empowerment of the individual, not just giving instructions so that a person can be useful in a particular job.
GROUP OF ASIAN DISABLED PEOPLE, LONDON

There should be integrated education for disabled and able-bodied children.
GROUP OF DISABLED PEOPLE, COVENTRY

I'd like hope for our children as far as the education system is concerned. They should bring back free school meals for all children, free milk and free uniforms. That takes the stigma away from children. There should also be an adequate supply of books.
GROUP OF LONE PARENTS, WALES

Leisure

Very few people spoke about the role of the welfare state in providing leisure facilities. For many, concerns about benefits, and other services essential to survival, seemed too great for them to think about leisure provision.

At the same time, leisure services have been an established part of state provision, with amenities like libraries, sports and recreational facilities provided through local authorities. The state also provides substantial funding for the arts. For those who did comment, and significantly this was women particularly, leisure services were important and were highly valued:

I'm an avid swimmer ... and like to still be able to go free ... because even paying once a week would be difficult.
GROUP OF OLDER WOMEN, LONDON

Libraries are constantly being cut back, some (rural) areas don't even get a mobile library now.
GROUP OF UNEMPLOYED WOMEN, GLOUCESTERSHIRE

I'd like to be able to go to the theatre regularly, and be able to pay whatever price I feel able to pay ... I feel education and leisure is not as good as it should be.
GROUP OF OLDER WOMEN, LONDON

LEISURE: THE FUTURE

The Commission deliberately focussed on people for whom the welfare state was particularly important. It is perhaps not surprising, therefore, that leisure did not figure as central to participants who were having to think mostly about managing on a low income or securing the essential support to live their life on a day-to-day basis. However this could give a false impression of the importance of leisure provision as an aspect of public and welfare policy. Publicly provided leisure services are likely to be of particularly significance to people on low income and other groups who have restricted access to the private sector.

Themes for the future

As well as offering their views and proposals for specific welfare state policies and provision, participants in the Commission explored a number of themes in their discussions and individual evidence. Some of these were raised by specific questions which we asked. Others they generated themselves through their own interests and concerns. We have grouped them together because all have important implications for the future of welfare. These themes are:

- revaluing people who use welfare state services
- service users' contribution to the welfare state
- waste in welfare
- paying for the welfare state
- the importance of employment
- information and access to services
- redress when things go wrong
- welfare for the future.

We shall look at each of them in turn.

Revaluing people who use welfare state services

While the welfare state was intended to guarantee people's citizenship and provide safeguards to counter the risks, injustices, hardships and problems of life, the reality seems to be that use of its services, especially its income maintenance service, has become a badge of second class citizenship. This was one of the strongest messages communicated in the evidence we received.

The devaluing of welfare state service users

One of the issues most often raised by welfare state service users who gave evidence, and one that engendered some of the strongest feelings among them, was the indignities which they experienced as recipients of welfare. For the majority of people who spoke with us, receipt of welfare went hand in hand with powerlessness, demoralisation and stigma. This was a view which was widely shared across groups of service users. This is how most people expressed their experiences:

I don't think you can feel valued on benefits.
GROUP OF TEENAGE MOTHERS, LINCOLNSHIRE

Unemployed people and people in low paid jobs aren't respected. They're treated as a commodity or an annoyance. They are not valued.
GROUP OF UNEMPLOYED WOMEN, GLOUCESTERSHIRE

You actually become the stigma and you become stuck in a rut with no way out.
AFRO-CARIBBEAN GROUP, MIDLANDS

It's demoralising to actually feel you're on it (welfare). That's what I feel the problem is.
GROUP OF EX-DRUG USER PARENTS, SHEFFIELD

I think a lot of problems of society stem from unemployment. Most people want a job and can't get one, they've got so little to live on, and they get depressed and end up on anti-depressants. Sometimes they commit suicide. There's a high crime rate as well. I think all that could be put down to unemployment. For people who are on the dole and depressed, they just need something to do.
GROUP OF UNEMPLOYED PEOPLE, YORKSHIRE

They seem to think you chose to be on the dole.
GROUP OF YOUNG PEOPLE FROM UK

If you're made redundant or lose your job they just don't want to know.
GROUP OF PEOPLE ON LOW INCOME, WALES

The worst thing is that they've made people feel they are not part of society. Other people think, 'We're better than you. We can provide for ourselves. You can't. Go away', so it implies it's for others, not everybody.
GROUP OF UNEMPLOYED WOMEN, GLOUCESTERSHIRE

I've been working for 30 years and now, all of a sudden, I've got to

rely on the state. When I went to the benefits office, they made me feel so small, but I thought, 'Bugger this. I paid for this for 30 years. I am entitled to it!'
GROUP OF PEOPLE ON LOW INCOME, WALES

I think I have managed to lower my expectations, both for my own life and for social change.
MALE MENTAL HEALTH SERVICE USER RECEIVING BENEFITS, SHEFFIELD (28)

When I went to sign on I felt pretty degraded ... We're only seen as dossers.
GROUP OF EX-DRUG USER PARENTS, SHEFFIELD

You get these MPs who do nothing but belittle the population – single parents, unemployed and people on the sick. You know, there's plenty of people who are working who do worse. They work second jobs. They don't pay any taxes.
GROUP OF PEOPLE ON LOW INCOME, WALES

You've got upper class, middle class and working class people then you've got this other class of people, like myself as a lone parent, who have no way to raise their standard of living.
GROUP OF LONE PARENTS, WALES

Some people felt so powerless that they saw no point in participating in the Commission. After one group discussion an unemployed man said to the worker:

I didn't say anything because there is no point. Nothing will happen. Nothing will get better or ever change.

For others, their experience of welfare was so oppressive that they could only explain it in terms of social control and regulation. For example:

It's all about controlling the masses.
AFRO-CARIBBEAN GROUP, MIDLANDS

I think that the whole emphasis has been taken off people to get up and to go and do something themselves, they've set up a whole society of people nowadays who've got no choice but to sit down and watch telly or go out and thieve.
GROUP OF EX-DRUG USERS, SHEFFIELD

There is a long-term plan – it's to keep the buggers down.
GROUP OF UNEMPLOYED WOMEN, GLOUCESTERSHIRE

The benefits system is a form of oppression. It's a barrier between the upper class and the lower class, they're just trying to keep us down.
GROUP OF YOUNG PEOPLE FROM UK

Participants condemned policy which forced unemployed people into work:

You're given a choice, take this job or lose your benefit. If you take the job you end up in something that bores you, it's too hard or not suitable, or you don't get on with the people, whatever, and you end up leaving the job, and you can't get dole for six months. Either way, they're getting you out of the system for six months to a year. Give me the chance to go to college and let me get the job that I want to do and then I will bother to keep a job and I will work harder than anybody else to keep my job.
GROUP OF YOUNG PEOPLE FROM UK

Some participants saw the closure of the free Benefits Enquiry Line for claimants, at the same time as a new hotline for reporting benefit fraud was introduced, as epitomising the stereotyping of people on benefits as lazy and scroungers by politicians and the media:

They got rid of the free line because they 'couldn't afford it', but they've got a free line to shop your neighbours – in other words we're all scroungers.
GROUP OF UNEMPLOYED WOMEN, GLOUCESTERSHIRE

I also feel people should not be made to feel guilty for living on benefits or anything else. The 'cheatlines' resemble the situation in Nazi Germany.
STUDENT (32)

Many people believed that their situation and many of the shortcomings of the welfare state arose because there was a lack of understanding of what it was like for people who live on benefits:

The people in government haven't got a clue of what it's like to be on benefits. They're on £50,000 a year and they haven't got a clue what it's like to live on £100 a week.
GROUP OF LONE PARENTS, YORKSHIRE

We elect the politicians to oversee the system, but they don't then

*listen to the community. They don't listen to our needs. Why do we
need a Citizens' Commission and all these other watchdogs? We're
watching people in power who should be ensuring that people
receive the support that they need.*
GROUP OF PEOPLE LIVING WITH HIV/AIDS, MANCHESTER

Specific groups also had particular concerns about the way they
were treated by the welfare system.

Young people

Young people rejected their ineligibility for benefit between the ages
of 16 and 18:

*It's just bare-faced-cheek ... a kick in the nuts that 16 to 18 year olds
can't claim dole.*
GROUP OF YOUNG PEOPLE FROM UK

Minority ethnic groups

People from minority ethnic groups felt that their entitlement to
welfare state services was frequently challenged unfairly on the basis
of their ethnicity and origins:

*We have little recognition as citizens of the United Kingdom. Many of
us came to this country a very long time ago, and during our prime
have made an enormous contribution working in all sorts of areas, but
many feel that they are not entitled to welfare benefit.*
GROUP OF ASIAN DISABLED PEOPLE, LONDON

Disabled people

Disabled people were seen as particularly vulnerable to being
pushed out of mainstream society by welfare:

*If it hadn't been for the relatives and friends a lot of disabled people
would be shoved in a home.*
GROUP OF CARERS, YORKSHIRE (D)

Carers

Carers were critical of the terms on which support was often given to
them:

*You sometimes wonder why they bother to give you help. They don't
seem to care for you as people.*
GROUP OF CARERS, YORKSHIRE (B)

The attack on service users as part of the attack on welfare

Instead of offering people security and acting as a safety net in society, the security which welfare itself offered had declined and it is now actually adding to people's insecurity:

There used to be security of knowing that you can't go any lower than a certain point and the welfare state would always be there for you if you fell on hard times. But now they're changing the criteria all the time and you don't know whether you are going to quality and you're always insecure.
GROUP OF LONE PARENTS, WALES

Some participants thought that some politicians and media were deliberately promoting the idea of the welfare system and its users as a burden:

Young people are made to think that (older people are a burden) because that's always in the media, all the time talking about the burden of old people, so people's opinions are being manipulated.
GROUP OF OLDER WOMEN, LONDON

I think that the government uses us as a scapegoat to take the blame for their fuck-up. They seem to try to blame everything that's going on in society on people using the welfare state and there's a lot of ignorance because people believe what the papers, the telly and the politicians say. The only good thing is that people are starting to realise it's not necessarily true.
GROUP OF YOUNG PEOPLE FROM UK

Some saw a clear agenda underlying these views.

They are out to get rid of (the welfare state) ... and they try to make a 'them' and 'us' situation and make tax-payers think, 'Why should we pay for these people?'
GROUP OF UNEMPLOYED WOMEN, GLOUCESTERSHIRE

From the perspective of service users the attacks on the welfare state and on its recipients seemed to be closely interlinked. Condemning one had the effect of condemning the other. Participants felt that both attacks were divisive and destructive, for broader society as well as people who needed benefits and welfare services:

We're trapped with no jobs, no pension, no future.

It's going back to Victorian ideas of deserving and undeserving people in need.

GROUP OF LONE PARENTS, WALES

The future of this country frightens me. It is no longer a decent, humanitarian society.

WOMAN STUDENT, LANCASHIRE (10)

Participants felt that the perception and treatment of service users had to improve if there was to be a future for welfare.

If we were valued by the welfare state it would look after us better.

GROUP OF CARERS, YORKSHIRE (D)

People should receive the services they are entitled to. These are not things the community is asking for free, because people have made their contributions in the past.

GROUP OF ASIAN DISABLED PEOPLE, LONDON

This required a change in culture and social attitudes, as well as practical steps forward. Some participants thought that at the heart of such reform, there needed to be greater involvement for welfare users in the system:

Maybe we should have a committee made up of different organisations, with somebody representing single parents, somebody representing pensioners and so on. They would then know from their own experience what people need and say how much we get.

GROUP OF LONE PARENTS, YORKSHIRE

Service users' contribution to the welfare state

We have already heard about the contribution which service users want to and do make to welfare state services through their knowledge and expertise, by getting involved in and informing its policy and provision. They also talked about the financial contribution they made to the welfare state.

In much of the current debate about the future of welfare, the 'tax payer' in employment has tended to be presented as paying for the system and its sole contributor. This is one of the sharpest and most destructive expressions of the way in which the dominant discussion about welfare has been framed in terms of 'them' and 'us'. 'Us' are the wealth creators who pay for welfare; 'them' are the wealth consumers who receive it. In this version of welfare, at best, welfare state service users are portrayed as taking from the system without making any contribution; at worst as parasites and scroungers intent on sucking the system dry.

Service users pay taxes too

Participants in the Commission challenged this over-simplified analysis. While their isolation and powerless did make some people feel that they made little or no contribution to the welfare state, others rejected this interpretation. They made it very clear that they were tax payers like everybody else:

> Please stress in all you publish and distribute that we ALL have a giving role at some stage of our lives, and nobody is ONLY a 'giver' or ONLY a 'receiver'.
> ELDERLY WOMAN (44)

> Don't forget that everyone's paying in things like VAT, so just because you're on benefits it doesn't mean that you're not paying.
> GROUP OF LONE PARENTS, WALES

> But we all pay taxes. We all pay VAT when we're shopping, that's tax.
> GROUP OF DISABLED PEOPLE, COVENTRY

> It is fallacious to depict service users, most especially the elderly, as parasites battening on to a long suffering, abused and neglected state. The National Insurance scheme is exactly what it purports to be: the insurance scheme whereby one pays in when one can.
> DEAF, UNEMPLOYED MAN (46)

> I smoke a lot, so I contribute a lot there!
> AFRO-CARIBBEAN GROUP, MIDLANDS

> We would like to see a welfare state which recognises that pensioners are not a useless burden and still play a valuable role in society....without them Britain would not be what it is today.
> ELDERLY MAN, STAFFORDSHIRE (45)

The increasing emphasis in UK taxation policy on indirect rather than direct taxation gives added force to this view. The introduction of new taxes like VAT on fuel has also been particularly punitive for people on low income.

Many older people had a strong sense of having made their contribution while they were in employment:

We paid our insurance in the old days which paid for a lot of things, including our pension, and we feel we've paid.
GROUP OF OLDER WOMEN, LONDON

Others made a similar point.

Many of us have paid our taxes in the past. I have worked all my life and in my last ten years of working, I helped run a medium size business which paid a fortune in tax.
GROUP OF PEOPLE LIVING WITH HIV/AIDS, MANCHESTER

Ways people contribute

In addition to their role as tax payers, participants identified a number of other ways in which they contributed to the welfare state. Many people felt that having to live on benefits was itself a consequence of the contribution they were making:

I gave up (my job) to look after my father-in-law, so I think I've done my bit in that way and now I'm saving the welfare state a lot of money by looking after him at my house instead of moving him into a home where it would cost them a lot more money.
GROUP OF CARERS, YORKSHIRE (D)

We're staying at home to look after our kids, so we're actually saving the government on nursery places.
GROUP OF LONE PARENTS, GLASGOW

They spoke of other ways in which they felt they played their part. Several people highlighted the work of volunteers:

I think that volunteers and others are all working for nothing ... so surely we're helping the government because we're saving them a vast amount of money by doing the work for nothing.
GROUP OF OLDER WOMEN, LONDON

There's a lot of unemployed people who do voluntary work, they save the system millions, but that's not recognised by anyone.
GROUP OF UNEMPLOYED WOMEN, GLOUCESTERSHIRE

The evidence of welfare state service users themselves offers a helpful corrective to the conventional polarisation of people into creators and drainers of wealth; welfare producers and consumers. Not only did the service users who gave evidence to the Commission highlight the contribution they were already making, they also stressed and made clear that they wanted the opportunity to contribute more in the future:

We're unemployed workers, not unemployed people, and once we get back into the system we will contribute even more.
GROUP OF UNEMPLOYED WOMEN, GLOUCESTERSHIRE

One young man who was homeless pointed out that if the welfare state helped him at this time in his life, he could then make a contribution later in life:

As a young person, I am at a crucial point in my life. The important thing for people of my age to do is to study and get qualifications and the welfare state should help me to do this. If it doesn't help me to do this now I will never get off of the benefits. If it helps me now I can then make my contribution later.
GROUP OF YOUNG HOMELESS PEOPLE, LONDON

Waste in welfare

The wastefulness of welfare has been a major theme of political and media debate. Welfare has been attacked for its inefficiency, bureaucracy and for supporting people who should be paying their own way. When we asked people in the group discussions whether money and resources could be better used, many thought that they could, but they generally placed a very different interpretation on this to many politicians and newspapers.

The inefficiency of policy by cuts

They condemned reforms which were supposed to cut costs but which increased them. Some participants highlighted the way in which spending cuts to make short term savings were actually leading to waste and inefficiency in the long term:

Everything's short term. If they helped us to get into work with a more flexible system it would be more cost effective.
GROUP OF LONE PARENTS, WALES

They've cut back so much in health and education that the people they're paying to do the jobs aren't even able to carry out the function they are being paid for, which isn't good use of resources.

They cut back one area and create more use of other services. There's no long term plan and it costs more in the long run.
GROUP OF UNEMPLOYED WOMEN, GLOUCESTERSHIRE

They criticised privatisation and the contracting of services as poor use of resources:

They've got these agencies based in the Job Centres signing people up for jobs. Why should we need these agencies when that's what the Job Centre should be doing?
GROUP OF PEOPLE ON LOW INCOME, WALES

Some welfare state service users argued that the Family Credit system wasted resources as it supported employers to pay low wages. For example:

Employers should pay a reasonable wage, then you would save the government an awful lot of money.
GROUP OF PEOPLE ON LOW INCOME, WALES

Some offered personal experiences of what they saw as poor use of resources. A lone parent receiving housing benefit suggested, 'It wouldn't have cost them nearly as much to give me a council (house)', compared with the amount of housing benefit that was paid to her landlord.

Abuse of welfare?
The idea that resources were being unfairly targetted at or being taken advantage of by some sections of the community was taken up on a few occasions during the Commission's discussions, but these views were usually challenged, as happened in this short exchange between three lone parents in Glasgow:

Some money should be taken away from services, especially the ones (with problems that are) self-inflicted.

You've got to consider, whatever your feelings, is this all right me saying this kind of thing ... especially if you live next door to junkies ... It makes it hard to have a nice liberal view on what kind of services they should get ... and you've still got to think of the children.

I think once it gets to a certain stage the addiction takes over and it's not a question of being at fault at that stage.

Paying for the welfare state

The improvements which people giving evidence suggested to deal with waste could result in savings, but welfare is still an immensely costly public policy. If we put to one side ideological objections to welfare, the main question mark that has been placed over it is how is it to be paid for. This has been a key concern of politicians, many of whom argue that the UK cannot afford to pay for the level of provision traditionally made.

Welfare state service users took a different view. Some saw the cost argument as irrelevant. Instead they saw the issue as one of priorities:

We were a bankrupt economy when the welfare state was started in 1945, and now we're told we've got a thriving economy, so why can't we afford it now when we could in 1945?
GROUP OF OLDER PEOPLE, WOKING

I'm not convinced that there's not money available. Look at the Falklands and the Gulf War, they found billions then.
GROUP OF DISABLED PEOPLE, COVENTRY

The need for us to have a welfare state must be better understood and it must be made a priority. When people say we haven't got the resources for the welfare state, we should be demanding that the money is found. You've only got to think of the Gulf War. When they told Maggie Thatcher we didn't have the money for it she said, 'Well find it' and they did because it was her priority. We need to make health and welfare the priority, then the money will be found.
GROUP OF OLDER WOMEN, LONDON

Investing in employment

There was also a widespread view that less unemployment would mean that more people could contribute to the system through income tax and that there would be less demand for benefits. Two carers offered this assessment of the current situation:

I think privatisation has caused a lot of this trouble. They put more people on to the streets, thousands of people out of work and they now depend on the state. They're on the dole and they can't contribute to the system because they have nothing ... If they were all working, they would be paying their stamps and income tax, but they're not, through no fault of their own. They're just walking the streets.

I think technological advances are also responsible for a lot of unemployment. For example, car manufacturing used to be quite labour intensive, but now robots are doing a lot of the work. There are not enough people working to support the vast hoards of people who are not working.

GROUP OF CARERS, YORKSHIRE (A)

Other participants had similar views, stressing the need for investment in employment:

One of the reasons there isn't enough is because there aren't enough people in work to provide the income to fund the benefits system. If there were more people in work, there would be less people needing benefits and more money there to pay a decent living wage to the people who are on benefits.

GROUP OF UNEMPLOYED WOMEN, GLOUCESTERSHIRE

You need to put more money into industries to create more jobs because then you've got people paying taxes and National Insurance and it all goes towards benefits and the National Health Service. If you're just going to throw money into the system you're wasting time. You could create an awful lot of employment just by re-introducing social housing.

GROUP OF PEOPLE ON LOW INCOME, WALES

We need more jobs and less people on the dole and a clampdown on all waste. We also need partnership reforms, some tax rises with some reductions in spending.

UNEMPLOYED PERSON, LONDON (7)

However there was also a sense that not all new jobs were improving the situation:

A lot of new jobs are part-time and people pay very little income tax if they work part-time.

GROUP OF CARERS, YORKSHIRE (D)

The role of taxation

Many participants saw taxation as a fair way for people to contribute to the welfare state:

> At the end of the day, the people who are well off should be paying more taxes. I would be prepared to do that.
> GROUP OF EX-DRUG USER PARENTS, SHEFFIELD

> I'm never in favour of higher taxes but something has got to be done in that line.
> ANONYMOUS (24)

> They say there's not enough money, yet they give tax cuts to workers. If I was employed and had children, I would be happy to pay more tax to give them a decent education.
> GROUP OF PEOPLE LIVING WITH HIV/AIDS, MANCHESTER

Some participants suggested that taxation might be more fairly structured with a greater number of tax bands. Another idea was that tax could be targeted, with people given the option to pay extra tax for specific areas like the National Health Service:

> I think that targeting income tax would help. For instance, if you asked for an extra tuppence that was specifically to go into caring or the health service, I'm sure that the majority of people would be happier putting money into that rather it just going into overall tax.
> GROUP OF CARERS, YORKSHIRE (A)

This idea was expanded by a carer from another group, who suggested a referendum:

> Ask people what extra they would like to pay for the welfare state ...
> I think it would come through.
> GROUP OF CARERS, YORKSHIRE (D)

Increased VAT was a popular idea with some participants, particularly on 'luxury' items. Older people seemed especially keen on this idea. There were also suggestions that funds from the National Lottery could be channelled directly into the welfare state and some participants criticised its use on what were seen as costly elitist arts projects, like the redevelopment of the Royal Opera House:

> I know the arts adds to the quality of life, but not as much as food in

*a baby's mouth ... I think first things first and the basics of life come
before anything else.*
GROUP OF CARERS, YORKSHIRE (D)

Saving resources

There were also ideas about how current resources could be better
used. One person believed that better use of resources would
remove the need to increase taxes:

*I think the tax payers pay enough money to fund the welfare state. We
pay taxes right, left and centre as it is to pay for a decent welfare
state. I don't know where all the money goes to. I would like to know.*
AFRO-CARIBBEAN GROUP, MIDLANDS

While the economy and effectiveness of universal benefits has been
highlighted, some participants questioned the value of benefits like
Child Benefit which are paid to rich and poor alike, on grounds both
of cost and principle:

*How can someone on £50,000 a year be claiming Child Benefit? I
mean, it's ridiculous, isn't it?*
GROUP OF EX-DRUG USER PARENTS, SHEFFIELD

*Some money, like Child Benefit, is paid to everyone whatever they
have and it goes to people with money just as it goes to people
without. If it was saved and just given to those who needed it, there
would be more money available.*
GROUP OF CARERS, YORKSHIRE (B)

Some participants also expressed concerns about benefit fraud. For
example:

*If they could cut out the abuse there would be more money for the
honest ones.*
GROUP OF CARERS, YORKSHIRE (D)

*People who abuse the system should be penalised in a way to make
sure that they don't do it again.*
GROUP OF PEOPLE LIVING WITH HIV/AIDS, MANCHESTER

They should have a crackdown on fraudulent claims.
GROUP OF DISABLED PEOPLE, COVENTRY

Others were unhappy with this emphasis on fraud:

*It's a bit obscene for disabled people to be talking about other
disabled people making fraudulent claims.*
GROUP OF DISABLED PEOPLE, COVENTRY

People stressed that the emphasis should be placed on serious
fraud and that this should be tackled in such a way that it did not
put people off claiming who were entitled to. Inadequate levels of
benefit forced some people into fraud and focussing on it diverted
attention from the real problem.

Some participants pointed out that while tax fraud was a bigger
problem than benefit fraud, it was not treated in the same way:

*People on benefits are treated as criminals for fraud, but it's seen as
legitimate to avoid paying taxes.*
GROUP OF UNEMPLOYED WOMEN, GLOUCESTERSHIRE

*We're always talking about benefit fraud, we should be talking about
fraud on the tax system.*
GROUP OF DISABLED PEOPLE, COVENTRY

Reallocating resources

Changing public spending priorities and reallocating resources was
seen as another important way in which funding could be found to
pay for the welfare state. Almost everybody said funding should be
cut from arms and defence budgets in favour of welfare spending:

Cut heavy spending on the military.
GROUP OF YOUNG PEOPLE FROM UK

We waste millions and millions on nuclear weapons.
GROUP OF OLDER PEOPLE, WOKING

Expenditure on the monarchy was also seen as wasteful by some
people:

Stop giving money to the Queen and give it to us!
GROUP OF YOUNG PEOPLE FROM UK

*What about taking a bit of money from lords and peers and royalty?
Some of them have millions doing nothing.*
GROUP OF EX-DRUG USERS, SHEFFIELD

Another area of comment was excessive salaries:

Mega salaries are totally unrealistic. If they gave everybody a decent wage, a minimum wage, everybody could live a lot better.
LESBIAN MOTHERS GROUP, GLASGOW

There are too many people getting big handouts, too much brass and too many fat cats.
GROUP OF CARERS, YORKSHIRE (B)

Not paying for the welfare state

Several people turned the question of paying for the welfare state around to ask:

How can we afford not to have a welfare state?
GROUP OF LONE PARENTS, WALES

Surely the question is how can we afford not to have a welfare state? If you don't give people money they are going to go out and commit crime to feed their families. I would if I couldn't feed my children because I had no benefits, I would commit crime to feed them.
GROUP OF UNEMPLOYED WOMEN, GLOUCESTERSHIRE

Dismantling the welfare state would lead to social tension and riots. To protect the welfare state is to protect freedom.
UNEMPLOYED PERSON, LONDON (59)

One lone parent had a clear vision of the action which needs to be taken to ensure that the welfare state is paid for:

There's no question of the system being too expensive. You have to afford it because if you don't have some sort of system you'll end up with civil unrest and everything in panic. The problem is that the government is handling it wrong and they need to take a long term view. Rather than taking 1p off income tax as a bribe to the electorate they should be saying, 'Come on folks, let's sort things out. The next five years are going to be hell on earth. We're going to put up taxes and sort out education and everything.' We're intelligent enough to know that whatever we do there's going to be a cost. The question is whether people are prepared to pay the cost.
GROUP OF LONE PARENTS, WALES

The importance of employment

Employment has been presented by government as the solution to individual reliance on welfare. The evidence of welfare state service users highlighted the need for an effective employment policy alongside an imaginative welfare policy. Blaming individuals did not seem an adequate alternative to them.

Almost everyone who took part in the discussions held by the Commission stated that having a job was important to them. Sceptics might argue that they would be bound to say this and that what they say and what they do are not necessarily the same. But the terms in which people spoke, and the determination underpinning what they said, suggest otherwise. For example:

It's a matter of self-esteem and self-gratification, having a feeling that you are going somewhere and earning your own living rather than having to keep taking.
GROUP OF EX-DRUG USER PARENTS, SHEFFIELD

More important than life.
UNEMPLOYED MAN, BIRMINGHAM (63)

I spoke to somebody yesterday who was ringing round Job Centres in London and Grimsby and other places. If that is not evidence of wanting work, then I don't know what is.
GROUP OF UNEMPLOYED WOMEN, GLOUCESTERSHIRE

I don't mind that they've cut my benefits. I know when I've finished this course I can go out and get a job.
AFRO-CARIBBEAN GROUP, MIDLANDS

There's loads of mothers like us who would like to get out and work for our money but we just cannot do it.
GROUP OF LONE PARENTS, GLASGOW

I would like a job where I live, but there aren't so I would have to go too far.
GROUP OF PEOPLE WITH LEARNING DIFFICULTIES, LONDON

There should be funding for training disabled people, because we don't just want to be sick and on benefit. We want training for employment so we can be independent.
GROUP OF ASIAN DISABLED PEOPLE, LONDON

I think it's important to be able to give. The situation we've been in, it's like you're constantly taking, and giving is quite an important part of everybody.
GROUP OF EX-DRUG USER PARENTS, SHEFFIELD

People who are on sickness benefit can sometimes work in supported work projects and thus fund some of their own benefit.
UNEMPLOYED WOMAN MENTAL HEALTH SERVICE USER, KENT (15)

If I could get a job, something with a reasonable wage, I could honestly say I would be a lot happier. I'm not working, I'm in the house 24 hours a day. Sometimes the kids have been playing up, being riotous, and you sit looking at the four walls, then you scream. So if I could just get out there and get back to work, it would benefit me and the kids.
GROUP OF LONE PARENTS, GLASGOW

I want people to respect that I have a disability, but that I've got services to offer.
GROUP OF DISABLED PEOPLE, COVENTRY

Throughout our inquiry, in the evidence submitted by individuals and in their comments in the group discussions, welfare state service users challenged the essential idea that people choose to live on benefits as a soft option. Two women summed up a general view:

People on benefits are very restricted. You have no independence.

Exactly. I don't want to have to look over my shoulder all the time.
AFRO-CARIBBEAN GROUP, MIDLANDS

Decent jobs, not work at any price

There has been increasing pressure on unemployed people to take any job, regardless of their experience, skills and qualifications. This reflects both the political concern to reduce the number of people included in unemployment statistics and the rising proportion of unskilled, insecure and part-time employment in the labour market. Many participants qualified their willingness to work by saying that they were not prepared to take any work on offer:

We want jobs with a decent standard of living, that pay a reasonable wage.
GROUP OF UNEMPLOYED WOMEN, GLOUCESTERSHIRE

I know some managers at (a well-known fast-food chain) and they're earning crap money. You're not getting any gratification ... and I'm not going to be a slave for someone else.
GROUP OF EX-DRUG USER PARENTS, SHEFFIELD

> *They want us to do jobs putting nuts and bolts in plastic bags … it's soul destroying.*
> GROUP OF DISABLED PEOPLE, COVENTRY

> *We need jobs that are actually paying a living wage. I mean, there are jobs if you look in the Job Centre, but what most of them pay you just can't live on. You're worse off than being on benefits in most cases.*
> GROUP OF UNEMPLOYED PEOPLE, YORKSHIRE

> *If you're doing something you enjoy, you may get somewhere, but if you get a job you don't like, you get bored and end up doing drugs.*
> GROUP OF EX-DRUG USERS, SHEFFIELD

> *They're pushing you to go into a job which you know nothing about.*
> GROUP OF YOUNG PEOPLE FROM UK

At the same time, participants who were in low paid jobs provided further evidence of people's willingness to work:

> *I claim Family Credit but I worked it out that I would probably be better off claiming Income Support, but then I would be a statistic, one of the unemployed.*
> GROUP OF PEOPLE ON LOW INCOME, WALES

> *I go out to work and maybe get a little above what I would get on social security. I do this because I want my independence and I want to feel that I'm contributing to my way of life.*
> AFRO-CARIBBEAN GROUP, MIDLANDS

Others offered reminders of the work they were already doing. People with child care responsibilities often felt that their role was under-valued in society:

> *I mean, who wants to be a layabout all their days? Maybe they think that's what it's like being a mother! It's a real job to me.*
> GROUP OF LONE PARENTS, GLASGOW

Carers made the same point:

> *I've got a job. I look after my wife. That's my job. That's what I get paid for. Unfortunately, all I get is £34 a week and after I am 65 I won't get paid at all, but how can I retire?*
> GROUP OF CARERS, YORKSHIRE (B)

Finding employment

While there is widespread recognition that high levels of unemployment are now a feature of UK and western economies, unemployed people are frequently expected to find their own individual solutions. Most participants felt there was a lack of recognition of the difficulty in finding work and challenged the view that work is there to be found by those who want it:

You have to travel to work (because of living in a small town) but there's little transport, and you can't afford what there is anyway, so it's a Catch 22 situation.
GROUP OF UNEMPLOYED WOMEN, GLOUCESTERSHIRE

There are black people out there that have left school and gone to college and worked very, very hard to get qualifications. But they go out there to find themselves a decent job to live the type of life they want and they can't get the jobs. I don't want to bring race into it but it is there.
AFRO-CARIBBEAN GROUP, MIDLANDS

I can't imagine getting a job. To get a job now you've got to be over-qualified.
GROUP OF EX-DRUG USERS, SHEFFIELD

Employers' attitudes to disabled people are very negative.
GROUP OF DISABLED PEOPLE, COVENTRY

People who have been unemployed for years have had all their initiative, self-will, and self-worth taken away, then they expect them to get a job.
GROUP OF UNEMPLOYED WOMEN, GLOUCESTERSHIRE

The role of government

Participants saw it as government's responsibility to create employment:

More jobs. They should create more jobs for lads that are coming up now and cannot know what it is like to have a wage.
GROUP OF OLDER PEOPLE, YORKSHIRE

The aims of the welfare state should be to provide a decent living for people who cannot work. Alternatively for the people that can work, to

find work for them, but paying a decent wage that people can be
expected to live on.
WOMAN, YORKSHIRE (35)

Some participants found it difficult to reconcile the scale of unmet
need with high levels of unemployment:

There are thousands in need of housing, many builders are out of
work, and thousands of properties awaiting repair in my area. Why
are the builders not working on those properties to house the
thousands?
WOMAN, YORKSHIRE (40)

One person identified what he called 'a cultural problem' with
current employment patterns that needed be changed:

We have a section of the population permanently on benefits and in
public housing and others in permanent employment. Life on the
dole should not be 'normal'. There should be more flexibility in work
available: temporary, part-time, casual.
MALE MENTAL HEALTH SERVICE USER RECEIVING BENEFITS,
SHEFFIELD (28)

Others saw a part for government to play in creating employment,
which would then also raise taxation income and help pay for
welfare:

We need to pay for the welfare state through taxes, through
investment and particularly through investment in people in this
country. I know of one company that actually sends its typing out of
the country.
If there were more people in work, there would be more people to
pay the taxes so they wouldn't have to be so high.
GROUP OF PEOPLE LIVING WITH HIV/AIDS, MANCHESTER

Information and access to services

Many people who gave evidence to the Commission had had very
poor experiences of trying to find out about and obtain services.
This applied particularly to community care, although it also
extended to some other valued welfare state services. A large
number of carers and disabled people had struggled for years
without support which they had needed and to which they were

entitled. Carers seemed to have considerable difficulty in getting support, and many got it by chance or because they had reached a point where they could no longer cope on their own:

The welfare state is a secret! If there is a welfare state, it's a well kept secret. I was a carer for ever such a long time before I knew that there was any way you could get any sort of assistance.

I had to have a nervous breakdown before I found out the help available.

GROUP OF CARERS, YORKSHIRE (B)

The day that I said I would do no more, that I would not come home to help again, was the day we began to get attention. As long as you carry on, they just let you get on with it.

I don't think the welfare state's ever supported me.

GROUP OF CARERS, YORKSHIRE (C)

Disabled people have had similar experiences, as this discussion between members of a centre for independent living shows:

There's an awful lot of people who are not aware of a lot of services that are available to them. Their social worker should have put them in the picture, but if they don't people are left to find out about these things for themselves and that means that services must be accessible. At the moment things are just too complicated for a lot of people and it all becomes a bit hit and miss.

Yes, you end up with a situation where you're all right if you speak to the right person at the right time, but if you don't, you've missed it.

You end up just hearing about things by word of mouth, and it shouldn't be like that.

You only get services if you push for them, but you've got to know that they're there to ask for them.

GROUP OF DISABLED PEOPLE, COVENTRY

People living with HIV/AIDS talked about the difficulties which they can face:

It's been a long job for me getting the services I require, but I am pretty confident and I was able to ask and make enquiries. I am used to being able to do that, but most people who have just been diagnosed and are getting over the shock, just don't know what to do. What worries me more than anything is that there are many people

who need health and support services who are losing out and are
outside the system. It almost seems that this is a way of rationing
services and limiting numbers.
GROUP OF PEOPLE LIVING WITH HIV/AIDS, MANCHESTER

Having to ask for help posed particular problems for older people:

The way we were brought up the problem was your own, and you
find it very, very hard to ask for help. You feel really guilty that you
asked for help.
GROUP OF CARERS, YORKSHIRE (B)

Members of minority ethnic groups reported continuing direct and
indirect discrimination when they tried to obtain services:

They came to my home to assess my wife for home help and they
say, 'We have such a lot of foreigners that there is a long wait for
services.'
GROUP OF ASIAN DISABLED PEOPLE, LONDON

There's no interpretation for black people the way there is for the
Asian community, but a lot of our older folks still speak the home
language.
AFRO-CARIBBEAN GROUP, MIDLANDS

Former drug users talked about the difficulties they had experienced
accessing rehabilitation services to get the support they needed:

(The rehabilitation project) was something we had to search for and
write away and pick people's brains, because information just isn't
available, it's only if you really search for it.

It's like going through hell. We had to apply through social services
and the community drugs team and none of them would put up the
money unless we showed a really high level of needing it. They
made us feel really bad because we needed to apply for it.
GROUP OF EX-DRUG USER PARENTS, SHEFFIELD

Improving access

The ideas welfare state service users had for improving access to
services mainly related to improving the availability of information.
For example:

Information should definitely be available through the family doctor.
GROUP OF CARERS, YORKSHIRE (B)

If you leave hospital with any type of impairment, you should be given a pack which gives you all of the information on services that are available.
GROUP OF DISABLED PEOPLE, COVENTRY

You should be able to go to somebody and say, 'Right, what do I do about this' and so on.
GROUP OF CARERS, YORKSHIRE (B)

If English isn't your first language it is very hard to obtain certain information. There should be more information provided to people in all walks of life, of what is available. This could be done through the media, workshops regionally with interpreters, signers for deaf people, equipment for blind people etc.
WOMAN, LONE PARENT, BRISTOL (17)

Efforts to improve information and increase access to services are often criticised for increasing demand for limited and finite supply. But by this argument, all services are subject to rationing and this cannot be done rationally and effectively unless people know what they are entitled to and can seek to obtain it.

Redress when things go wrong

In any organisation or system, things can sometimes go wrong. The consequences in welfare, where people may be without money or in urgent need, can be catastrophic. Provision is needed to deal with such difficulties. In both the National Health Service and social services, complaints procedures were introduced by law. Yet when we asked people about complaining, it was clear that existing arrangements were generally inadequate. Not only was complaining often difficult, especially for people at what might be particularly difficult or vulnerable times, when they might feel in a weak position, but some thought that the system was reluctant to treat its users fairly when things did go wrong. For example:

You go to your MP, you go to your social workers, you go to your doctors, and at the end of the day you're still in the same situation because nobody hears us, so who do you go and scream at? Nobody wants to hear us.
GROUP OF LONE PARENTS, GLASGOW

Getting them to accept they've made a mistake in the first place is difficult enough.
GROUP OF UNEMPLOYED WOMEN, GLOUCESTERSHIRE

They say 'Yes sir, leave it with us' and you go away and never hear nowt.
GROUP OF CARERS, YORKSHIRE (B)

They (social services) protect their own back. It's internal, so it's all hushed up.
GROUP OF LONE PARENTS, WALES

Participants in rural areas had particular difficulties making complaints:

You've got get on the bus (to get to the benefits office) and you've got no money to do that. It's ridiculous.

You rely on that Giro from that date to the next date, for your electric, for your food, for everything. If they make a mistake and the Giro doesn't come that day, you're without money. But you go to that office and try and explain that you are without money and they just don't understand. They turn round and say, 'You can go to Gloucester and get it'. I ask, 'How do I go to Gloucester when I've got not money?' and they say 'Sorry, you'll have to wait till tomorrow'. So you go through that day without anything.
GROUP OF UNEMPLOYED WOMEN, GLOUCESTERSHIRE

Another woman in the group followed this up:

In that situation you access the social services for emergency funding, but even that's getting more and more difficult, because they're cutting their budget but getting more people asking for help.

One resident of a hostel for homeless people in London was able to report a positive result from making a complaint:

I had been for an interview about benefits and just because I said that I was homeless and living in a hostel he started to talk down to me and said he wouldn't do any more about my claim. He got all funny with me and just blunt answers to the questions I asked him. I think he thought that if I didn't get any help that I would just go away and not come back, but I made a complaint and then they realised I was serious about it. I don't know how far the complaint went, but the way I was treated at my next interview was perfectly fine

because they knew that I wasn't going be messed around and they
sorted my claim out then and there.
GROUP OF YOUNG HOMELESS PEOPLE, LONDON

Participants in the Commission thought that complaining could be made easier with better information about procedures:

Everyone should be given a pamphlet regarding complaining, giving
a step-by-step guide. It could be in the back of the pension book,
then you would have it whenever you needed it.
GROUP OF CARERS, YORKSHIRE (D)

But as we have already seen, what most felt was needed first was that welfare service users should be routinely treated with respect as equals, rather than devalued as inferiors.

Welfare for the future

One of the supplementary questions which we included in our schedule for group discussions asked participants their views about the welfare state in the future. But service users raised what they wanted for welfare in many different parts of their discussions. They had clear ideas about what they believed the welfare state should be doing in the present and the future. They emphasised its role in providing security, independence, quality, empowerment, equity and equality:

The welfare state should be there to pick up on anyone in need.
GROUP OF PEOPLE ON LOW INCOME, WALES

Welfare should be the responsibility of the entire state.
GROUP OF ASIAN DISABLED PEOPLE, LONDON

There should be a minimum standard across the board, a minimum
standard that is acceptable for a civilised society.
GROUP OF LONE PARENTS, WALES

Health and education are probably the most important areas that they
should put money into to have a strong population.
AFRO-CARIBBEAN GROUP, MIDLANDS

Providing a decent quality of life and decent quality education and
medical treatment for everybody in Britain.
LESBIAN MOTHERS GROUP, GLASGOW

I am independent at the moment but would like the welfare state to be there as a safety net if I am unwell or unemployed.
WOMAN, KENT (25)

The welfare state needs to grow and empower people rather than decrease and disable them.
UNEMPLOYED WOMAN, NOTTINGHAM (26)

To give people a chance to achieve their aims and ambitions and not be made to feel like a statistic
MALE STUDENT, SHEFFIELD (64)

I strongly believe that we all have to accept that we all require respect, we require dignity and we require independence to the best of our ability. But too often now, we have to go cap-in-hand to charities. We're being made to beg, but we are not beggars. We just want what is rightfully ours. I don't just say that for people living with HIV, but for everybody.
GROUP OF PEOPLE LIVING WITH HIV/AIDS, MANCHESTER

There is a concept of the welfare state where we give opportunity to everybody to develop their potential to the maximum and we ensure that people have a minimum of facilities.
GROUP OF OLDER WOMEN, LONDON

Things have been going downhill. The fact that all people should have equal access to education and health and have a basic living is what a welfare state should be about.
ANONYMOUS (24)

I see the welfare state as something that will give equality for all people irrespective of whether they're working, unemployed, sick, have a disability or mental health problem. Everybody will have equal opportunities to get what they deserve, a right to live happily and healthily.
GROUP OF OLDER WOMEN, LONDON

I want to see socialism – human need rather than capital interest – being the driving force in society. Let us reintroduce the notion that people's health, livelihood, and needs are the primary concern of a responsible government. We need to do this firmly so that this notion will be established for good, not tokenistically, as this will lead to its being removed again.
MAN PREVIOUSLY UNEMPLOYED, KENT (11)

The most important thing is for the welfare state to be available to all who need it and not just those who the government considers deserving.
UNEMPLOYED DISABLED WOMAN, KENT (60)

The criteria for the welfare state should be to be provide security, because insecurity affects everybody, from homeless people through to the well-to-do people worried about their homes being repossessed.
GROUP OF ASIAN DISABLED PEOPLE, LONDON

For me security is the key thing, whether it is employment, benefits, housing, whatever. There's insecurity all around. You just don't know what's around the corner and this breaks up communities because everyone's watching their back. I'd like to see the next generation have the best security in employment and in knowing that if they became ill, lost their job or whatever, there is a safety net.
GROUP OF LONE PARENTS, WALES

One service user who completed a questionnaire, suggested that a Bill of Rights should set out minimum standards for welfare (43). This related to a broader theme in the evidence: that service users should have more say in welfare. It emerged particularly strongly in the context of community care, where some progress has already been made:

It is important the welfare state listens to the needs of the elderly.
ELDERLY WOMAN, SURREY (1)

People participating in the Commission saw a need for major changes:

If we're going to have a shake up of anything, we need a shake up for the young. Give them some hope for the future. There's none at the moment. They come out of the schools and there's nothing whatsoever for them.
GROUP OF PEOPLE ON LOW INCOME, WALES

They raised the need for far-reaching change in both policies for the welfare state and in attitudes towards it. But there were concerns that such change would be difficult:

My biggest worry about the welfare state is how difficult it's actually going to be to reverse the changes because the damage has been

done and it's going to be very difficult to get public support for future governments if they want to reverse the changes. We're in a no win situation.
GROUP OF LONE PARENTS, WALES

I don't think anybody can look forward in the confused state we're in now, always asking where is this coming from, where is that coming from? In five years time I'd like to see us get ourselves sorted out.
GROUP OF CARERS, YORKSHIRE (A)

Some felt that to protect and improve the welfare state would involve looking beyond the system itself, as part of a broader re-examination of economic and employment policy, as well as social policy:

We should get away from old concepts of employment and unemployment and go over the welfare state so that people are given the opportunity to use their creativity. We have our own capacity and yet we are having to fit into a very little slot of what is called a 'job'.
GROUP OF ASIAN DISABLED PEOPLE, LONDON

There's lots of things they could do to regenerate the economy and generate more income. They've sold a lot of the council houses but they can't use the money from it. If they used it to build new housing, it would have a big knock-on effect. If you build houses you need roads, you need gas, you need electricity, you need glass, you need furniture and carpets and so on. So building houses creates lots of other jobs, so I think you could achieve a lot by stimulating house building.
GROUP OF LONE PARENTS, WALES

Not surprisingly, many people were despondent about the future and saw little hope for change. In discussion one lone parent, however, argued that welfare state service users would have power if they worked together:

We have to stand up and shout, not just about things for us as lone parents, but on other issues as well, such as disability. We should argue. We should go to our MPs. We should campaign. We have to say that this is the reality and we are not going to stand for it. But it's no use just blaming the government. They're just 650 MPs. We need to reach the population, the tax payers.

But we're still a minority.

We're not a minority. I think you can take this conversation into any group around the country with different views, but they will all have similar concerns to us. But how many people sit at home and look at the bad things and don't do anything? They say that one person cannot change the world, but I believe they can. One has a view and tells others, then they tell other people too and soon many people will hold that view and then things will change.

GROUP OF LONE PARENTS, WALES

It is this view which underpins the Citizens' Commission and this Report of its inquiry.

PART 3

Our future welfare

Pulling it all together

In this Chapter, we draw together the evidence which we received from welfare state service users, identify a series of key findings and conclusions which emerge from them and offer a set of recommendations following from their views and proposals.

What we learned from the Commission

We began this process, as we said in Chapter 3, by spending time at the final meeting of the Commission discussing the outcome of the inquiry.

This was to enable members of the Commission as a *group* to work out together what they thought had emerged from it. We talked about some of the initial findings from the inquiry identified by the Commission's worker. We also discussed our thoughts about the welfare state now and for the future, in the light of our experience and work on the Commission, meeting and talking with other welfare state service users and hearing what they had to say.

The views of members of the Commission closely reflected those of individuals and groups submitting evidence. This is perhaps not surprising. There was a remarkable degree of consistency in the evidence we received nationally: from different groups, people in different areas and people of different ages. While different groups and individuals had different priorities, the problems they identified tended to be similar and their overall ideas and proposals for change corresponded closely.

The welfare state today

In the light of their inquiry, members of the Commission raised a range of general and specific issues about the current state of welfare. The overall picture was of a system in crisis and collapse that could no longer meet the needs it was set up to serve.

I think there's a state of crisis. Access to services is becoming more and more restricted, particularly health services with longer and longer waiting lists.

People with mental health problems just do not get adequate services. Day care services leave a lot to be desired. There are waiting lists for day care which just should not happen. Even people in crisis situations are having to wait for somebody else to move on or die before they get any help. Residential care is also appalling. They just say that the money isn't there.

Social services are often bad and don't provide a service to people with learning difficulties. Housing is very poor, but the council takes no notice and they say they haven't got the money to do the repair, but they have money for lots of other things. People are not treated equally.

The government is secretly dismantling the welfare state. They say they are not, but I think they are, but we all need pensions and the health service.

A lot of people find themselves worse off working. It happened to me. I found a job and came off Income Support and went on Family Credit and by the time I'd paid my rent and council tax, I was £44 a week worse for working, so they should stop taking Family Credit into account when working this out.

As they say, older people are having to pay for residential care three times over. First they are taxed when they are working. Then they pay tax on their pension and then they are having to sell their homes to go into residential care and they are very, very frightened. They are terrified.

The biggest joke is the new carer's right to an assessment. I can go to my husband's consultant, GP or whoever and say I am very tired and need some respite, or that I need a stairlift, and they would do the assessment, but then there is no money available to pay for anything that I am assessed as needing. Carers are only worth £35 a week through the Carer's Allowance, but we save the government £56 billion a year.

Problems with pensions

Commission members shared the concerns of welfare state service users giving evidence both about current pension levels and the availability of pensions in the future:

Everyone is very concerned about pensions and even the basic state pension is in doubt now. I have been working with pensioners groups to try and get some commitment from the political parties to the top-ups to the pension, but we've had no indications that any party will take this up. They say that the country cannot afford the 'demographic explosion' – the so-called 'granny bulge'. When people ask about the money that they have put in over the years and show them how they could afford to give a decent pension, they just won't be drawn.

Problems with privatisation

There were serious doubts about policies encouraging people to take out private pensions and other forms of private insurance:

Most of us are very innocent. I think that people knew when you had a state pension system that the government might not be very efficient, but they wouldn't rip you off and people go into private arrangements with the same view, but they do rip you off.

Private pensions are only open to people with a job and things like private health insurance exclude many people like disabled people. They won't take anyone who's a risk.

The whole idea of privatising welfare state services was called into question:

It's important to highlight that privatisation has caused many of the problems. Some of the privatised services are able to do things more efficiently, but surely that could be done without privatisation.

Problems with employment training

Concerns about privatisation extended to its application to training schemes for unemployed people. Commission members talked about the inadequacies of these:

On these training schemes, they do the same work as someone sitting next to them who's earning a proper wage.

A friend of ours did a Restart course. He's 52 and they showed him a video on how to get a job as a manager at Gateways (supermarkets). He made a joke of it and told the trainers that everyone in the video was 30 years younger than him and that there were no more Gateway stores in the city anyway. They'd all been taken over. But he said afterwards he felt really humiliated. Then he went on a computer course, but it's all run by private companies and so far out of three sessions, first, the tutor turned up and showed them how to start the computer and then went off, the second time he was off sick and the third, nobody knew where he was. They don't really care about the people they are training. They just want to keep the numbers up for their contract.

In one city, they put everyone on the training scheme for hairdressers.

How many hairdressers can they have?

Another Commission member had recently completed a training course for women returning to work and had been disillusioned by it:

There was nothing for us at the end of the course. It was just back to square one. No, it's even worse, because you had the dream before and that's been taken away.

This was seen as part of a broader trend of people's hopes and horizons being narrowed:

People are getting used to the idea of having to take a crappy job and everybody's expectations for their lives are going down.

Problems for children and young people

The situation of children and young people was another major concern of Commission members. One member summed up the current situation and the need for change:

It's inappropriate that children are entirely dependent on their parents. Society seems to deny any responsibility for children and leaves everything to the parent. Therefore if children have well-off and supportive parents, then they are alright, but if they don't, it's very tough on the children. It's down to the parents to fight for everything their child has and the more well-off the parent is, the more privileges the child gets, with a better education, easier access to health care and usually an all-round happier childhood.

There's no sense that children are the future of the country, the future workers and the future of society as a whole. I am not trying to deny the responsibility of parents, but the attitude is that children are only the responsibility of parents: that you've had them, so you should bring them up. I feel more and increasingly resentful of this attitude.

Issues for education

Commission members were also worried about how well young people were being prepared for life by the education system, for example in this discussion between three of us:

Children need to learn the basic survival skills of life. Education should teach children about homelessness, the Benefits Agency and life skills like cookery.

Isn't that a backward step? Should we be teaching kids about the Benefits Agency? It's saying that we're going to teach you this because you'll need it when you leave school. I would rather say at the end when you leave school there will be a job.

I know it sounds awful, but often there isn't one.

In a changing world, even more was required of education:

They don't know any of life's skills. (They) aren't doing woodwork and it's not being passed down from the parents because the parents are unemployed, so education should pick up on that.

The inclusion of disabled children in mainstream education was also identified as a priority:

Disabled children are still excluded from mainstream schools, as the policy of integration is being done on a shoestring, or is just not happening at all. Being excluded from the education system means that you're excluded from society. You are left with low expectations and other people have low expectations of you, so you are very limited in what you can achieve.

Some welfare state service users were still effectively excluded from society and the most basic human rights:

It denies people rights. It denies them citizenship. Some people with learning difficulties have never voted, never had a say. They are invisible citizens.

The Commission's findings

After discussing their own concerns about the welfare state, in the light of their work, members of the Commission examined the initial findings of the Commission identified by the worker. They focused on a series of problems which welfare state service users had highlighted and which needed to be challenged for things to improve. These were: the demonisation of welfare users; the denial of poverty and social problems; increasing social division, the individualisation of problems and responsibility and the inadequacy of services.

In a period when users of welfare have been made the scapegoat for many social ills, their direct evidence offers an important and overdue opportunity for reassessment:

> *The findings may be surprising to many people. They need to know that people on benefits are not just fraudsters and that we don't want to be in this position and would rather be in work than be having to ask for money. People who are not in this position just don't think about these things.*

> *What would people do if there wasn't a welfare state for them? I think people were worried about that.*

This led members to consider why there seemed to be so little public and political awareness of the rights and needs of people who use the welfare state and why so little action had been taken to tackle problems of poverty and unemployment. For example:

> *There's a hell of a lot of denial about poverty and people just don't want to believe that it exists. I've just moved into quite a wealthy area, but there are pockets of poverty everywhere, but it's often hidden. This was brought home to me doing the course for women returning to work and most of the women there were completely ignorant about the existence of poverty and their attitudes towards it help create and perpetuate the problem. They had this idea that people on benefits live really well.*

> *The politicians are a million miles away from all this and now they've got 'excuses'. You can do it privately. There isn't the money and never will be. Other people respond to things by just pretending they are not there. It makes me think it took a world war to get a welfare state. What would have to happen to get it back?*

> *The media encourages us to deny these problems. It talks about fraud more than anything else.*

Members of the Commission thought there was a strong message that problems were being individualised and that society was becoming more divided and that this helped explain the lack of action on poverty and other social problems. This was reflected in the following exchange between two members:

Everything has become very individualised and Maggie Thatcher is the person who is most to blame for this. Take community care. It's far from what it says it is. It's either poor older women doing the care, or people being shoved into hospitals that push you out too early. Everything's been individualised and it's the way the politicians keep us all apart so that they can stay in power. They want to keep people apart and not let us get together to help each other.

Yes, they blame us for our situation and they try to set us at war with each other.

Particularly on pensions as they say the young will be burdened with paying for us, so they are dividing young and old, yet opinion polls have shown that when young people are in work, that they are happy to pay for us.

They blame the pensioners. They blame the single parents. They want us to be at war with each other.

The Child Support Agency was seen as an example of this divisiveness:

It has taken away the state's responsibility to support single mothers and it becomes the responsibility of the partner. All that media stuff about what a burden single parents are seems to have paid off for them. We now remain tied to our ex-partners.

Meanwhile the support services which people had paid for and thought would be there when they needed them were collapsing:

An elderly man said he knows someone who needs help with a bath. He's very concerned because he also needs a bit of help himself. He's about 85 and there's some things he needs help with that they won't give him. Social services say they are trying to get the money to help people to get a bath. They are still trying to get money for it and he's not getting the help he needs.

The future of welfare

Members of the Commission were united in the belief that the welfare state must be maintained and improved. This was seen as a moral as well as political, social and economic issue:

There must be a welfare state. There are fundamental baselines which I believe we shouldn't cross. I think it is a moral argument. There are moral standards and people have to pay through their taxes. What kind of society would we have without this? I believe we don't just work and live for ourselves and that we do have a 'community'.

People need services and this modern philosophy that those who can afford it get services and those who can't, don't, is no good. It is not good for society as a whole to keep reducing the welfare state and make people destitute and homeless. It has become like a big tree with all the branches hacked off. Without a welfare state, people are also denied the chance to contribute.

Paying for welfare

They were in no doubt that it could be paid for:

The welfare state should be paid for by taxes.

Mainly it should be paid for by taxes. If you have more, you should pay more.

Like everything else (it should be paid for) by taxes, using people's money either as a (direct) tax payer or consumer.

People have paid in all their lives, but the government has reduced benefits and pensions. Services have been cut back and people have to pay for what they get. People's money has been hijacked by the government. The welfare state should be a mechanism to control greed, but government seems to have promoted it.

Members of the Commission recognised that it might be difficult to persuade current and future governments to put resources into the welfare state and suggested:

We should have more information on budgets and how the money is spent, then we could have more of a say in things.

I can only see that people want a welfare state and a health service and they are willing to pay for it, as long as they see what they are getting.

Getting the support we want

Members of the Commission, like welfare state service users more generally, were not just calling for more of the same. Welfare for the future had to be different. It had to offer good quality services, be accountable, safeguard people's rights and provide the kind of support that *they* wanted, rather than what other people thought they needed:

> *We need to look at the quality of services. At the moment the attitude seems to be you are lucky to get anything at all and quality is often very poor. We're often working so hard to get any services that quality just gets forgotten. Why should people with mental health problems have to accept hostel accommodation because there is nothing any better? Why should an old person with incontinence have to make do with a bath just once a week?*

> *I really do think in this day and age – we're going into the next millennium – we ought to be starting thinking of better quality care ... Why should people who are very vulnerable have to accept poor quality standards?*

> *I don't really want to go back to what we've had in the past, which was dependency creating. What I think is important is (disabled) people being given control over their own care arrangements.*

One member talked about her experience of special boarding schools:

> *They never sent my letters on to my parents. I wrote them and they never sent them. I didn't know that till I got home to my parents.*

Others highlighted the problems of abuse that have emerged in recent years:

> *More is coming out now about the level of abuse that has gone on in places like this ... These places were shut off and people had no rights at all.*

> *How the hell do these paedophiles get in these jobs?*

Commission members wanted to see universal services maintained:

The trend seems to be that only the very, very poorest will get benefits and yet while most people are not that poor, we still need benefits because we have a disability or being a carer and so on. We need to try to maintain the universal benefits that we have and make sure that welfare state benefits help everybody in need and do not just become a net to catch those most in need.

Benefits should be reintroduced for 16 and 17 year olds. People need money at this age and that's why you get all this crime. Not having the money affects their health and some turn to drugs. Bringing back these benefits would also save money on policing and young offenders institutes. Even on the training schemes they don't give them enough money.

They also wanted welfare to respond to people's different needs sensitively and under their own control. One disabled member of the Commission pointed to a new example which offered a model for the future, beyond traditional state paternalism and the new for profit market – direct payments:

We have an opportunity for this with the new law allowing councils to make direct payments (to disabled people to run their own support schemes). I think that direct payments and the support infrastructure around that are very imaginative and will produce the kind of welfare state we want. We want a welfare state where the service user is an integral part. The user is the controller and the person who creates the structure – part of the fabric of the whole. But direct payments must be supported and resourced properly and users involved.

Commission members saw economic regeneration as the way to achieve this and create the welfare state that people wanted:

Get these empty buildings going. Get the unemployed working and making those things that we used to, that we're bringing from abroad. That would be more money into the taxes and there wouldn't be so many relying on benefits ... There would be money for the schools and the hospitals that are falling down.

Findings and conclusions

The overall picture of welfare emerging from is users its alarming. It shows a system which was intended to provide some security in people's lives which now compounds their insecurity. It is a complex and contradictory picture, rather than a simple one. There is evidence of waste and inefficiency in welfare's organisation, while vital 'life and death' services are grossly underfunded or non-existent. The scale and degree of suffering for many welfare state service users is unquantifiable.The report from the front-line truly is of a system in chaos. We begin with two important introductory findings.

The consistency of the findings

Welfare state service users have clear and consistent things to say. The Citizens' Commission was established to enable welfare state service users, for the first time, to have a say in discussions about the future of the welfare state: to contribute their experience, views and proposals. Users of welfare have increasingly been blamed for many of the problems that exist in society. This makes it all the more important to hear their side of the story. There not only seems to have been some reluctance to involve them in the discussion, there also appear to have been doubts that they would be able to contribute or have anything helpful to say. The findings of the Commission make it clear that this argument cannot be sustained.

The wide range of people who submitted evidence provided positive confirmation that recipients of welfare state services not only have an essential contribution to make, but they are quite capable of offering it. Participants in the Commission were able to report their experience clearly and in detail. They had views to offer about the present and the future of welfare and their proposals were rooted in the practicalities and realities of their day-to-day experience of welfare. They offer a unique perspective on welfare policy, practice and philosophy, which is an essential complement to political and professional contributions.

What was also striking about the evidence of welfare state service users was its remarkable consistency. As we would expect, different individuals and groups had different focuses and emphases of concern and interest and there were some disagreements. But overall, the experience, concerns and hopes of different groups, young and old, black and white, women and men, in town and country and different parts of the UK, were very similar.

Inquiry between equals

An inquiry based on welfare state service users being able to take part on equal terms with people with shared experience and understanding, made possible a fuller and franker understanding of welfare from the perspective of service users. The Commission's approach to its task was based on a clear philosophy of welfare state service users taking their own initiative and finding out for themselves. This was a self-run initiative, not a top-down inquiry. Such a participatory approach to research and inquiry is relatively new and is still challenged by more traditional approaches, which question its validity, reliability and independence. All these concerns can be answered. While the approach is innovatory, it rests on established principles and well-proven methods. It can make also a strong claim to independence. The Commission was unrelated to any political party or position, left, right or centre, and was not associated with any professional or institutional interest.

But the Commission's work also showed that its approach had its own significant and particular strengths. The fact that Commission members and its worker were themselves also welfare state service users, offered important gains of its own. A different, fuller picture seemed to emerge because welfare state service users felt they were being talked to at the same level. In both individual evidence and group discussions, participants were remarkably frank and open. We know from some comments that they made, that one reason for this was that they knew that they would not be stereotyped, judged or devalued by the Commission, because of our shared experience. The Commission offered a safe opportunity for people to express their views, talk about their experience and offer their hopes and ideas, where they could know that they would not be patronised, ridiculed or looked at askance. The value and importance of this cannot be overestimated at a time when welfare state service users are constantly under attack and debate about welfare is defensive, heavily politicised and ideologically loaded.

Independence not dependence

Independence was a key theme emerging from the Commission's enquiry. It was expressed by all groups of welfare state service users. Both direct service users and carers emphasised its importance. They wanted the support that they needed to live their lives independently and for people to be able to contribute to each other and to society. They were not offering a simplistic idea of people 'standing on their own two feet', but of people having the wherewithal to participate in and be active members of their communities and society. Many felt *trapped* in the welfare system and they wanted ways out of it. They saw themselves caught in both a benefits and poverty trap and an opportunity trap, which made it extremely difficult to live their lives and contribute as they wanted to. Their idea of independence had three expressions. People talked about support for people to live independently and not:

- be pushed into, or kept in institutions or segregated in special separate services because of old age, ill-health, disability, mental distress and so on, but to have the right kind of support to live their lives as fully as possible, like other people;

- have to rely on partners, family and friends to 'look after' them if they were disabled, frail or distressed, but for suitable, flexible, good quality support and services to be available when needed;

- have to rely on benefits to live, but to be financially self-supporting, primarily through access to properly paid, good quality employment.

This is a crucial finding. It also turns conventional wisdoms about welfare and its users on their head. While welfare state service users have increasingly been stereotyped as 'dependent' and 'disaffiliated', they make it clear that the opposite is the case: that they are desperately trying to challenge the pressures which push them outside society and on to reliance on poverty level benefits.

We can expect that there will be some people among welfare state service users who don't want paid work or to help others, just as there are in every other group. But the clear message from these findings is that this stereotype cannot be applied to most people who use welfare. The real issue that emerges is not welfare service users' 'lack of responsibility', but their desire not to be forced into and kept in dependency. What also becomes clear is that the economic and welfare reforms of recent years have actually made this problem much worse. They have forced more and more people into reliance on welfare who don't want to be.

Cuts in welfare services are forcing more responsibility on to unpaid carers, yet this inquiry offers further confirmation that this is an oppressive and unworkable policy. Many carers are themselves old. They and the people they support are denied choice and frequently left in poverty, without adequate support. Disabled people and other social care service users highlighted that they wanted to live an ordinary life and that this included equal opportunities for paid employment. This raises a key problem with current and traditional approaches to welfare which its users identify.

It is mostly concerned with supporting people *outside* the labour market, rather than enabling their participation within it. For some groups, like disabled people and people with learning difficulties, this has been because regardless of their abilities, they have not been seen as suitable candidates for employment. For lone parents it has been linked with the lack of suitable and affordable child care. For others, it follows from the contraction and restructuring of employment, leading to massive increases in long term and regional unemployment and low paid work.

Welfare state service users saw employment as a right and not just an obligation. Many were currently denied this right. They wanted the same choices as others, including the choice of a decent job. While the debate about welfare has frequently been framed in terms of getting people into employment who are unwilling or unable to work, welfare state service users under conventional retirement age, made it clear that they wanted to be in paid work. They saw employment as a solution, not as a problem. Conventional commentators on the welfare state, particularly of the right, have tended to present employment as a social obligation. Service users made it clear that it would be more appropriate for it to be understood as a right and entitlement. The provision of paid employment was seen as a priority for individual welfare state service users and for government policy. While governments stress individual responsibility to work, they do little to help in terms of creating employment and perpetuate the exclusion of some groups. For example, the last government argued against an anti-discrimination act for disabled people and only introduced weak legislation, although it would increase disabled people's employment opportunities. Government has given priority to the interests of the labour market, for example topping up low wages with benefits, rather than to the interests of people who want proper paid work.

But participants distinguished between good quality employment and work at any price. They wanted employment which offered security and pay which would take them out of poverty and the benefits and poverty trap. They wanted decent jobs. Employment was valued as a preferable alternative to being on benefits. People did not want work which kept them in the benefits system. This has clear implications for government economic and employment policy. Policy based on low paid, unskilled and insecure employment will not offer welfare state service users a way out of welfare. Nor in the long run will it make possible a reduction in welfare spending, unless government plans for reductions in public expectations and standards of life. Instead policy must be based on the development of good quality employment offering an income above poverty level.

Some service users had a relatively narrow view of what welfare meant, focussing particularly on benefits and support services. It was not clear why, but it seemed to be linked to the run-down of welfare, particularly of 'universalist' services which were intended to be available to all. What it means is that there may no longer be a common language about welfare. Many other service users, however, took a much broader view. They wanted a return to the original goals of the welfare state, support to those above retirement age, sick or otherwise unable to work and temporarily excluded from the labour market, but with the main emphasis on positive employment. It was clear that welfare and employment policy are inseparable and must be considered together.

Service users wanted the good things from the old days of welfare, including reliability, security, as well as services free at the point of use, linked with good things that have developed more recently and which they themselves have often been involved in shaping, like more say, more choice, more sensitivity to people's diverse needs and provision, challenging oppressions based on 'race', age, disability, sexual identity, gender, class and so on.

The alternative they pointed to was increased access to good employment through a skills-based labour market, with increased education and training opportunities for people to gain skills which would be helpful in the economy.

They saw the way to pay for the *good* things from the welfare state was by making it possible for people not to have to be dependent on the *bad*, like means tested benefits and dependence. They offered an alternative approach to funding, based on taxation from creating good quality employment, which would then pay for the support people wanted and needed.

Paying for welfare

Discussions about the future of welfare have so far been dominated by the question of how to pay for it. They been overshadowed by political and expert judgements about cost. Usually these discussions have been narrowly framed, without taking into account other broader costs, human, social and economic, which may come into the equation.

It is essential to include welfare state service users in these discussions, otherwise their proposals can be dismissed as a 'wish list'. Their first hand experience of and expertise about welfare also mean that they have a unique and essential perspective to offer. Welfare state service users generally have a good understanding of financial realities and restriction. Not only are they particularly likely to have experienced these in their own lives, living on low income, they have also frequently encountered difficulties in accessing services and support because of the constraints operating on them. It is unlikely to be helpful therefore to begin with any assumption, as policy makers often seem to have done, that service users would fail to appreciate or understand that resources for welfare are and necessarily have to be finite.

Welfare state service users believe that the costs of welfare can and should be met by them being shared. For example, older people should not be expected to meet the cost of long term care. Welfare should be paid for by taxation. This is the right and most effective way of funding it and safeguarding people's wellbeing and security. They base this view on several key principles:

- *People are not asking for something for nothing*. They have paid for welfare in direct and indirect taxation, National Insurance, through unpaid work as carers and in many other ways. The conception of welfare in terms of two groups of people, those who pay for it and those who benefit from it, cannot be sustained. It is damaging and destructive and ignores the contribution of welfare state service users themselves.

- *Securing the future of welfare demands a change in political priorities*. The priority given to resourcing the welfare state needs to be reassessed in relation to other policies and services, like road building and defence. The funding of the welfare state is and always has been a question of political priority and human values. The National Health Service, pensions, long term care, education and other welfare state services must be seen as having high priority.

- *Much more attention needs to be paid to what the costs will be **without** the welfare state*. While the welfare state has its own costs, running it down and not having it, has many others. As well as the costs in terms of social disruption and community breakdown, which politicians frequently highlight, welfare state service users evidence many others, including ill health, mental breakdown, appalling poverty and people being unable to contribute to society through employment, for want of personal assistance, child care and other essential support.

Now we move on to the rest of the findings that emerged from the Commission's enquiry.

The importance of benefits *and* services

The debate about welfare has mainly focussed on benefits. They make up the largest part of the welfare bill and have been the subject of high profile political and media attacks for creating and perpetuating 'dependency'. While welfare state service users who gave evidence to the Commission had much to say about benefits, they also talked at length about welfare state services. These included health, community care and education services and public transport. People's lives were not compartmentalised along the lines of the administrative and departmental divisions that exist between benefits and services. Welfare state service users offered an important reminder that welfare services are no less important than benefits and that benefits and services are interrelated and need to be given equal consideration alongside each other. It is unhelpful and unrealistic to approach them in isolation. They highlighted the need for an *holistic* approach to welfare if effective and practical strategies were to be developed for the future.

The negative experience of welfare

Service users' experience and views of the current welfare state were generally very negative. This applied across benefits and services, including health, education and social services. While there were exceptions, they reported practice and provision which was of poor quality, inadequate and stigmatic. Benefit levels were singled out for particular attention as being grossly inadequate for people to live on. The benefits system was frequently humiliating and degrading to use. While service users were highly critical of the existing welfare state, however, they were certainly not arguing for its run down or replacement. Many highlighted that their lives would be much worse without it. Their criticisms of the welfare state were different to those which usually receive coverage and which have been associated particularly with the political right. While participants did identify some long term problems with the welfare state, most of the concerns they expressed related to cuts and changes which have been made as part of more recent right-wing reforms.

Excluded as second class citizens

However destructive the material difficulties were that welfare state service users described, they were only one part of the problems that they faced. People also expressed strong feelings of being disenfranchised and disempowered. People's exclusion from the welfare state debate was just one expression of this. They felt they had little or no control politically, socially, economically and often personally over their lives. For example, people who used the social and community care systems talked about their daily difficulties with them. They were unreliable and inadequate. Carers couldn't count on support. Older people could not be sure of getting the help and support that they needed. People felt victimised by the way the welfare system worked, made into second class citizens and denied their part as full members of society. The problem of social exclusion emerges as much more than that conceived narrowly in terms of people not being integrated into society through paid employment.

The reality of welfare

While expert and political discussion about welfare has tended to focus on the principles underpinning it and how to pay for it, in their comments welfare state service users paid no less attention to the way in which the welfare system actually worked. This concern with practical policy is hardly surprising since it impacts so directly on their day-to-day lives. They have unrivalled first hand knowledge and experience of how policy and principles actually work out in practice. This is another reason why their neglected perspective is so important and needs to be drawn into the debate. Their knowledge offers insights into how policy is actually being implemented. This has long been a missing link in the welfare policy-making chain. Welfare state service users' experience makes it possible, for example, to see how current principles of a 'mixed economy of welfare' and privatisation are working out. The results are not encouraging. There are few if any signs of problems under the old system being resolved, but rather of new problems being created. They reported inadequate, unresponsive and frequently unreliable treatment from both the benefits and the service system. They also talked about broader failings, for example of Family Credit and to provide support for disabled people and carers.

The importance of education and training

Welfare state service users see education and training as the route out of welfare. Both are currently inadequate. Many children and young people are not receiving an education which equips them for the difficult world which they face or which ensures them equality of opportunity as adults. Their opportunities for adult, further and higher education have been increasingly restricted by cuts in public spending. Government employment training schemes for adults and particularly for young people have conspicuously failed to secure most young people a place in the labour market. They have not offered valued skills and qualifications. They have not provided young people with a foothold into skilled and valued employment. Participants in the Commission were particularly concerned about the training and educational opportunities of children and young people since they represent the future.

Inadequate information

Welfare state service users identified lack of information as one of the key obstacles in the way of gaining the support which they needed and to which they were entitled. While the debate about welfare has increasingly focussed on its 'overuse' by people who should be 'standing on their own two feet', the evidence received by the Commission highlighted the problem of people being denied access to support and services to which they were entitled for want of accessible, reliable and independent information. This applied to both welfare benefits and welfare services. As a result, service users often didn't know what was available, what their entitlements were, or what choices and alternatives were possible. Frequently, at a time when things were likely to be difficult and they were feeling vulnerable, they would therefore face additional difficulties and strains. Carers talked about having to look after loved ones with no support, until by accident or in desperation they had found out about the provision that should have been available. Disabled and older people reported similar problems. Members of minority ethnic groups identified the lack of appropriate and accessible information as one of the factors which denied them full and equal access to the welfare state.

More say in welfare

One of the main problems of the welfare state which service users identified was that it was frequently insensitive, unresponsive and unaccountable to them. They felt they generally had little say or control over it and how it treated them. As a result they were often treated carelessly and badly. The worst treatment participants reported was by the benefits system. In their experience it was often inefficient and unpleasant. Increased reliance on quangos without formal democratic structures exacerbated problems. Existing provisions for redress in both welfare benefits and service systems were inadequate. Most experience of complaints procedures was negative. Participants wanted to have more say in welfare for the future. They saw this as an important way in which it could achieve its objectives more effectively. They did not want to go back to the welfare state's paternalistic past, where other people made decisions for them, frequently resulting in people having little say in their lives, often living in institutions and being offered segregated services. They wanted to have a real say in the service and support which they received. This has already begun to happen in community care, for example with direct payments schemes enabling disabled people to take control of their own personal assistance schemes. Increasing the say of service users was seen as an important way of ensuring that future welfare state services were of good quality, flexible and appropriate.

Wasting resources

Service users stressed the need for welfare state funding to be used more effectively and efficiently. Welfare reforms since the 1980s had placed much emphasis on 'value for money', reductions in waste, bureaucracy and unnecessary public expenditure. In their evidence service users said that these reforms were *themselves* a frequent and major cause of waste and inefficiency. They highlighted this problem in the benefits system, National Health Service, education and community care. Cost-cutting calculated in narrow accounting terms, and an increasing emphasis on short-term policy, resulted in false economies which ended up costing more. They also caused service users much hardship and suffering through lack of adequate and appropriate support services. Reorganisation, restructuring and the introduction of the 'purchaser/provider split' had resulted in an increased emphasis on managerialism, resulting in a shift of funding from direct service provision and a large rise in the number of managers.

Welfare users under attack

While people receiving welfare services frequently reported the negative treatment they received at their hands, this seemed to be linked to much broader social and public attitudes and values. Continuing political and media attacks on welfare state service users has clearly cast them in negative terms. Whether deliberate or not, the effect of right-wing rhetoric about welfare 'spongers' and 'layabouts' has increased the burden that people have to bear who need to turn to benefits or services, making some people reluctant to seek support however desperate their circumstances. Its effect has also been divisive. While social issues like unemployment, ageing, disability and child care, clearly play a key part in people needing to seek state financial and social support, their situation has been framed more and more in terms of individual responsibility and blame. Attacks on welfare and on its users have been closely interlocked. A climate of fear and hostility has been generated around both. There needs to be change in public and political attitudes towards people who use welfare.

PART 4

The practicalities of the project

REFERENCES

Colin Barnes and Gill Thompson, (1994), *Funding For User-Led Initiatives*, London, British Council of Organisations of Disabled People and National Council for Voluntary Organisations

Peter Beresford, (1995), *'Voices From The Sharp End: Service users and the future of the welfare state'*, Community Care, 6–11 January, pages 20–21

Peter Beresford and Jane Campbell, (1994),*' Disabled People, Service Users, User Involvement And Representation'*, Disability And Society, Volume 9, Number 3, pages 315–325

Mee-Yan Cheung-Judge and Alix Henley, (1994), *Equality In Action: Introducing equal opportunities in voluntary organisations*, NCVO Publications in association with Family Service Units, London

Commission on Social Justice, (1994), *Social Justice: Strategies for national renewal. The Report of the Commission on Social Justice*, Vintage, London

Suzy Croft, (1989), *'Sharing The Wider Issues Of Poverty: Report of an EC tribunal of poor women'*, Social Work Today, February 16, page 19

Suzy Croft and Peter Beresford, (1990), *'Involving Poor People In Poverty Research'*, Benefits Research: The Bulletin of the Social Fund Project, April, pages 20–22

Wiltshire and Swindon Users' Network, (1996), *I Am In Control: Research into users' views of the Wiltshire Independent Living Fund*, Devizes, Wiltshire and Swindon Users' Network

John Hills, (1993), *The Future Of Welfare: A guide to the debate*, Joseph Rowntree Foundation, York

Bob Holman, (1993), *'Right Wrongs, In Brief: The Commission on Social Justice wrote to Bob Holman asking which issues it should tackle'. This is his reply*, New Statesman and Society, 22 January, page 23

Ruth Lister and Peter Beresford, (1991), *Working Together Against Poverty: Involving poor people in action against poverty*, London, Open Services Project/Department of Applied Social Studies, University of Bradford

David Marsland, (1994), *Let's Kill Nanny*, Open Space programme, BBC 2 TV, June

Kirsty Milne, (1995), 'Welfare Statement', New Statesman and Society, 27 January, pages 20–21

New Statesman and Society, (1993), 'The Vision Thing: Labour's new Commission on Social Justice must be free to think the unthinkable', editorial, New Statesman and Society, 15 January, page 5

Mike Oliver, (1996), Understanding Disability: From theory to practice, Basingstoke, Macmillan

Alan Stanton, (1989), Invitation To Self-Management, Dab Hand Press, Middlesex

Transport and General Workers Union, (1994), In Place Of Fear: The future of the welfare state, Transport and General Workers Union, London

George Yarrow, (1996), Welfare, Mutuality And Self-Help, The Association of Friendly Societies, London

APPENDIX A

Members of the Commission

Joan Croft
Stella Best
Jane Campbell
Peter Beresford
Sally Fox
Zelda Curtis
Rose Thompson
Brenda Joyce
Les Speakman
Alice Etherington
Vasant Shend'ge

The twelfth member of the Commission, an unemployed woman, had to withdraw.

Commission worker: Michael Turner

Group discussions undertaken

We made a commitment to the groups who took part in group discussions that we would maintain their confidentiality and not mention them or individuals who contributed to them by name. The groups are identified by location and to reflect the basis on which they came together.

Group of carers, Yorkshire (A)
Group of carers, Yorkshire (B)
Group of carers, Yorkshire (C)
Group of carers, Yorkshire (D)
Group of Asian disabled people, London
Group of disabled people, Coventry
Group of disabled people, Yorkshire
Group of people with learning difficulties, London
Group of people living with HIV/AIDS, Manchester
Group of young people from UK
Group of young homeless people, London
Group of ex-drug users, Sheffield
Group of ex-drug user parents, Sheffield
Group of older women, London
Group of older people, Woking
Group of older people, Yorkshire
Group of unemployed women, Gloucestershire
Group of lone parents, Wales
Group of lone parents, Glasgow
Group of lone parents, Yorkshire
Group of teenage mothers, Edinburgh
Group of teenage mothers, Lincolnshire
Asian support group, Lincolnshire
Lesbian mothers group, Glasgow
Group of unemployed people, Yorkshire
Group of people on low income, Wales
Group of people receiving benefits, Yorkshire
Afro-Caribbean group, Midlands

APPENDIX C

Individual evidence submitted

Some individuals submitted evidence on the questionnaires we distributed. Others provided it in statements, letters, phone calls and on tape. Some included their name and address; others contributed anonymously. We made clear to contributors that they could offer evidence anonymously. This was because of welfare state service users' widespread fears and concerns about negative repercussions if they offer any comment, particularly from the benefits system. The numbers we have attached to individuals are those we have used next to their quotes in the text to simplify identification. We have provided what information people gave us about themselves.

1. Elderly woman, Surrey
2. Disabled person receiving benefits, Wiltshire
3. Elderly person, Surrey
4. Disabled elderly man, London
5. Woman with chronic illness receiving benefits, Leeds
6. Disabled and unemployed person with experience of homelessness, London
7. Unemployed person, London
8. Unemployed homeless man, London
9. Elderly Asian couple, Middlesex
10. Woman student, Lancashire
11. Man previously unemployed, Kent
12. Woman, Kent
13. Woman, Greater Manchester
14. Elderly person, Staffordshire
15. Unemployed woman mental health service user, Kent
16. Woman, London
17. Woman, lone parent, Bristol
18. Older employed Asian man, Yorkshire
19. Young unemployed man, Bristol
20. Person originally from Latin America receiving housing benefit, London
21. Elderly man, Manchester
22. Woman, Lancashire
23. Elderly man supporting son with mental distress, who receives benefits, Middlesex
24. Anonymous

25. Woman, Kent
26. Unemployed woman, Nottingham
27. Black woman, Nottingham
28. Male mental health service user receiving benefits, Sheffield
29. Disabled person on benefits
30. Parent of disabled three year old
31. Woman, part-time student, Glasgow
32. Student
33. Student nurse
34. Anonymous, Yorkshire
35. Woman, Yorkshire
36. Lone parent, Yorkshire
37. Lone parent, Yorkshire
38. Anonymous
39. Anonymous
40. Woman, Yorkshire
41. Man, London
42. Disabled male student, Lancashire
43. Man serving life imprisonment, London
44. Elderly woman
45. Elderly man, Staffordshire
46. Deaf unemployed man, London
47. Middle aged disabled man, Kent
48. Man with experience of mental distress, West Midlands
49. Elderly man, member of ex-service men's association, East Sussex
50. Person with chronic illness
51. Elderly disabled blind man, Yorkshire
52. Woman carer with disabled son
53. Man, Belfast
54. Unemployed man, London
55. Elderly man, London
56. Male user of mental health services, Birmingham
57. Elderly woman, London
58. Woman carer of uncle aged 92, Surrey
59. Unemployed person, London
60. Unemployed disabled woman, Kent
61. Elderly woman, Surrey
62. Unemployed person
63. Unemployed man, Birmingham
64. Male student, Sheffield
65. Woman on sickness benefit doing voluntary work, Sheffield
66. Anonymous
67. Man on sickness benefit, Sheffield

APPENDIX D

Ground rules of the Commission

- We will all try to use simple language and not use jargon or initials when we talk to each other.
- If people need a break, they can feel free to leave the room for a break or a cigarette.
- Smoking is not allowed in the building where we are meeting. But if people want to smoke, there is a covered place at the back of the building as well as out at the front.
- We all try to make sure that everyone can have their say and we don't interrupt each other.
- If anyone talks about personal experiences, then we treat that as confidential and don't mention it outside the group.
- If we don't agree with something that someone says, then we say so at the meeting if we want to, but we don't take it up with them separately on their own.
- We own our own ideas. If we have an opinion then we are clear that it is our opinion and don't say something like 'Oh, a lot of people think such and such'. If it is someone else's view then we say whose it is.

Contract with *People First*

Agreement to be on Committees

If you want People First to be on your committee, you need to agree to this list of things first.

☐ We must have a <u>REAL</u> voice on the committee. We will not be on your committee just to make it look good.

☐ You need to explain to us clearly why you want us on your committee.

☐ You need to explain to us what People First will get out of being on the committee.

☐ Information, minutes, and agendas must be easy for us to understand.

☐ Information, minutes, and agendas must be put on tape if we need them to be.

☐ We can have a supporter that we choose. This supporter can help us in the meetings and outside the meetings.

☐ The supporter will be paid by you.

☐ Other committee members need to be trained about how to really involve us on the committee.

☐ The committee has to use words that we understand.

☐ We can stop meetings if we need to have something repeated or explained.

☐ We can have breaks in meetings when we need them.

☐ If the rest of the committee gets paid, then we get paid the same amount.

☐ You will pay for our expenses for the committee.

We would like to be on your committee if you agree to these things.

If you agree, please sign here.

_____
Name of the Committee

_____   _____
People First   Committee
                      Member

_____   _____
Date   Date

APPENDIX F

Commission worker: Job and person specification

1. What the worker needs to do: the job specification

- to help, support and focus the group
- to network and make contact with welfare state service users
- to pull the information we get together
- to write the Report of the Commission
- to arrange the meetings, both of the Commission itself and with service users more generally
- to keep notes of meetings
- to keep day to day financial records
- to be responsible for the Commission's letters and calls.

2. The qualities the worker needs to have: the person specification

- first hand experience of long term welfare state services/benefits and/or membership of a group for whom long term services/benefits are provided (for example lone parent, disabled person, unemployed person)
- to be plugged into relevant networks
- the ability to use a keyboard
- the ability to write reports
- good skills with people
- good organisational ability
- self-motivating and adaptable
- good understanding of and commitment to equal opportunities
- good abilities to facilitate abilities
- the ability to meet deadlines
- to be able to travel
- a personal commitment to the project.

Information pack: Undertaking group discussions with welfare state service users

Some information to help

We agreed to get together some information to help members of the Commission carry out discussions with other welfare state service users. Here it is. It includes:

- Introduction
- Some practical things we need to do
- Help notes for carrying out the group discussions
- What to tell people when we do the group discussions
- Ground rules for carrying out the discussions
- The Commission's equal opportunities statement
- Questions to ask people in the group discussions
- What the Commission means by the 'welfare state'

Introduction

We agreed to produce these notes to help members of the Commission and our worker carry out group discussions with welfare state service users. Remember they are meant to help – not to tell you what to do. When you are having a discussion, you'll be there and you'll be in the best position to know what is likely to work best and what feels most comfortable for you and other people. If you have any problems, please get in touch and we'll be pleased to help in any way we can.

Please read these notes. Hopefully they'll be helpful!!

They include some suggestions to help you carry out your discussions, some things to tell members of the group you meet with about the Commission and what we are doing, and the questions which we agreed we would ask.

Some practical things we need to do

There are also some other practical things. For example if people who take part in the discussion have expenses, we'll need to get invoices and receipts for them. The same goes for our own expenses. We may also have expenses for other things like interpreting and signing for deaf people. We'll need to keep a record of things like this.

We are planning to use a tape recorder to record our discussions. Please use standard C90 tapes. They will be easiest for transcription. Check that the tape recorder you use will pick up what people will say in such a discussion. You can do this by putting it about ten feet or three metres from you and speaking and see what you get. If it will do that ok, then it will probably be ok for a discussion.

If you can't get hold of a tape recorder, then let us know so we can try and sort it out.

When you have completed the discussion, please make a copy of the tape before sending it off. Don't forget if we lose a tape, we lose the discussion unless each of us keeps a copy of the discussions we have. If you need help with copying, please get in touch.

Please send the tape when you have copied it and we'll send it off to be transcribed.

Please provide information with the tape to say who the discussion is with, for example who the group is, approximately how many people there were in the discussion, where they are from, and when it was undertaken. It is also helpful to know if people are black and/or white, so we can be sure we are including black people and members of minority ethnic groups. It is also helpful to write down your thoughts about the discussion, things that struck you when you were there, any questions or other issues people raised off the tape. Please make sure you include a contact name and address and phone number so we can keep in touch with the people we speak to and send them a copy of the transcript of their discussion.

Help notes for carrying out the group discussions

Don't worry if you don't have time to ask people all the questions you want to. Just do what you can and don't feel you have to ask everything. It's much better for people to have the chance for a good discussion about some things than for you or them to feel rushed to get everything done. That puts everyone under too much pressure.

Don't forget, what we are really trying to do is find out what kind of welfare state services and benefits service users want for the future to live their lives the way they want to and to be the people they want to be. That's what we really want to give people the chance to tell us and the questions we ask are really to find this out.

Remember the tape recorder can only pick up one voice at a time. If people want to talk at the same time, just tell them this, then they'll realise that the important things they've got to say will get lost unless they speak one by one.

Don't worry if there are silences or it doesn't seem to go as you hope it will. Discussions can be like that. People may not be used to talking in this kind of situation and may be nervous. They will get more confident as the discussion goes on. Each discussion will help give us the whole picture. It doesn't matter if we only get a bit from any one discussion. If people are a little quiet try and get them talking about what they're most interested in and spend a bit more time on that.

If you ask a question and people don't seem to understand it or seem a bit confused, then try asking it in a different way and write down what you said as a reminder. Not all questions that look ok on paper work when you are talking with people.

Try and keep things as informal as possible. We are welfare state service users talking to other welfare state service users, not researchers or academics. Be yourself and say things the way you always do. This is our strength and it's why people will trust and respect us and want to talk to us.

If somebody tries to do all the talking or dominate the discussion, try and help other people get a word in. There are lots of friendly ways of doing this, for example comments like, 'Thank you very much for that really interesting comment. Now let's hear from someone else who hasn't said anything so far!' Keep it friendly, but remember that people will look to you to run the discussion and may need help from you to say what they want to say. Sometimes it's helpful if someone looks as though they want to say something, but haven't quite said it, to say something like, 'Did you want to say something?' or 'Was there something you wanted to say?', just to give them that chance and the confidence to speak. If they say no that's ok too.

If anyone behaves unpleasantly or in a discriminatory way to anyone else then we need to stop that happening and point out that we are having these discussions with ground rules to make sure people treat each other equally and so that we respect each other.

You are there to be what people call a 'facilitator' – to help the discussion take place. This means that what you are trying to do is make it possible for people to say what they have to say. That might mean that you have to help things to keep going and sometimes move things on, as well as making sure that you don't do too much talking yourself! What's important is to try and keep a balance – to remember you may need to step in sometimes to help people say what they want, as well as keeping quiet to make that possible.

If there are quite a few people or the discussion gets lively, you may need to raise your voice and speak loudly to get people's attention. You may not want to do this, but don't worry, if you make it clear why you are speaking up, people will understand and not think you are being bossy. So you could say, for example, something like 'Can I just have your attention for a minute? Thanks,' in a strong confident voice, when you need to. Try not to feel embarrassed.

If you feel nervous or are worried that you need to keep your eye on the tape recorder or aren't sure quite how to ask something, then say so to people. That'll help them understand and put them more at their ease. Once again they'll realise you aren't just a researcher trying to find out things from them, but another welfare state service user trying to help them speak for themselves. It's another reminder we are all human.

What to tell people when we do the group discussions

Telling people about the Commission

When we meet with people to have a discussion, it is helpful after we have introduced ourself just to tell them a bit about the Commission briefly, so they are in the picture. It is a good idea to do this, even if you have mentioned it to one or more members of the group before, to be sure that people are really clear what is happening and what it is for.

We can tell people that the aim of Commission is to give users of welfare state services a chance to say what kind of welfare state they want to see for the future and that we – the members of the Commission – are all users of welfare state services ourselves. The Commission is independent and is controlled by people who use welfare state services. We have money from the Baring Foundation and *Community Care* magazine. We have a worker who is a user of welfare state services and we will put together what people say in a Report to use for campaigning locally and nationally.

How we are finding out what welfare state service users want

You might also want to tell people how we are finding out what welfare state service users want.

We are having meetings with people like this one.

We are asking people to send in their views and evidence – we are asking both individual service users and groups and organisations controlled by welfare state service users to do this.

The worker will help us produce a Report based on what people say.

We will be sending groups like this a copy of this Report and keeping them in touch.

Our agreement with people we have discussions with

It will also be helpful for people we speak to if we explain carefully when we are having a discussion with a group of people the conditions under which we would like to have the discussion and check whether these are ok with people or they want to suggest anything else. These conditions are:

- What people say is confidential – we won't talk about it outside the meeting with them.
- We won't identify any individual in the Report and we won't mention the name of any group if people don't want us to.
- With people's agreement we would like to tape record the discussion because that is the best way of getting an accurate record of what people say. This will be typed out later by someone who also knows it is confidential and has nothing to do with welfare state services and we will send them a copy of this.
- We will send the group a copy of the Report from the Commission.
- We have some ground rules for carrying out these discussions to help everyone involved be able to contribute fully and equally. We hope these are agreeable for people for the discussion today. These are the ground rules:

Ground rules for carrying out discussions

We will all try and use simple language and not use jargon or initials when we talk to each other.

If people need a break, they can feel free to leave the meeting place for a break.

We will accept the majority decision about smoking in the meeting place. If smoking is not permitted where we are meeting, or the group decides against smoking, then participants should feel free to take a break for a cigarette if they want to.

We will all try to make sure that everyone can have their say and we don't interrupt each other.

If anyone talks about personal experiences, then we all treat that as confidential and don't mention it outside the meeting.

If we don't agree with something that someone says, then we say so at the meeting if we want to, but we don't take it up with them separately on their own.

The Commission's Equal Opportunities Statement

The aim of the Citizens' Commission is to ensure that people who use welfare state services have a chance to put forward their ideas and experience and say what kind of welfare state they want to see for the future. So far service users have had little chance to take part in the debate about the welfare state and the Commission aims to help this to happen.

This objective means that equal opportunities has particular importance for the Citizens' Commission.

The Citizens' Commission is positively committed to ensuring that it does not directly or indirectly discriminate in its own working practices, in its broader contact with service users and in its employment practices.

People have experienced and continue to experience discrimination in society generally and specifically as users of welfare state services (including carers) on grounds of 'race', gender, disability, class, sexual orientation, age, HIV status, religious belief and practices, national origins, family circumstances, trade union status and psychiatric status.

The Citizens' Commission is opposed to and will find unacceptable all discriminatory practices, attitudes and behaviour.

In order to ensure that this equal opportunities policy is carried out the Citizens' Commission will develop guidelines for its practice and monitor their implementation.

Questions to ask people in the group discussions

These are the questions we ask people after we have introduced ourselves and explained what we are doing. (see the notes, What to tell people when we do the group discussions)

We agreed what we wanted to ask people about and to have some general questions to ask them. As well as asking these questions, when people answer we may ask them to tell us a bit more about what they mean and give them a chance to say a bit more.

If the group we are meeting with is a group that people set up which meets regularly (rather than some people who have come together to meet us) then it will be helpful to ask them about themselves. For example we can ask them briefly about their group:

- What is your group called?
- What are the aims of the group?
- What sort of things do you do?

(This should help people be more at ease. Then we can go on to asking the main questions we agreed.)

These are the questions:

There is a lot of talk now about the welfare state.

- What do you think the welfare state is?
  Or: What does the welfare state mean for you?

  (We are asking people what they think the welfare state means but if they aren't sure or would like some information, then we can tell people what we think it means. This isn't so they have to agree with us, but just to give them some ideas to help them think about it.)

- What parts of the welfare state (services and benefits, for example education or income support) are most important or matter to you most?

- Why is this?

- What do you want for your own life, say in five years time – for the future? (for example how do you want to be living; what do you want to be doing; how do you hope things will be)

- How do you feel you contribute to the welfare state? (for example paying taxes on your income and what you buy, being a carer, bringing up children, having a job)

- What do you think makes for a good quality service?

- Do you think money and resources could be used better in the welfare state to be more sensitive to what people want?

- Can you give some examples of this?

- How could a welfare state in the future make sure that everybody is treated equally, according to their different needs, wherever they live and regardless of their 'race', gender, age, disability, class and sexuality?

- How do you feel you should be able to complain and get things right if they go wrong in the way you are treated as a user of welfare state services?

- How can welfare state services make people feel valued and not bad about getting them?

- How do you feel the welfare state can be paid for in the future?

- What do you feel is good about the welfare state now? What do you value in welfare state services and support?

- What do you feel is bad about the welfare state now? What do you feel are the problems and the bad things about welfare state services and support?

Here are also some additional things which it might be helpful to ask people. If there is time, try asking people these questions. You might also think of other things which you think it is important to ask people. The people you speak to will also have things they want to talk about.

- What do you think the purpose of the welfare state should be?

- What do you want for yourself and your life and for people in this group from the welfare state?

- What do you think it is most important that the welfare state does in the future?

- What do you feel would make it possible for you to live your life to the full and achieve your potential?
- Is having a job important to you? How could the welfare state help with this for the future?

At the end we can thank people and tell them again that we will transcribe the discussion and send them a copy of what they said which they can change or add to in any way they want to. Don't forget to get a contact name and address.

What the Commission means by the 'welfare state'

We have tried to work out what we mean by the welfare state, because it is not always clear. For us it means:

Being able to:
- be a full citizen
- to achieve your potential
- to have your rights.

It includes things like:

Benefits and pensions
Transport
Support services, like social services, community care, services for young and older people
Health care
Housing
Child care
Employment
Education, for children and adults
Leisure facilities
The environment.

We are also interested in how we pay for the welfare state. This includes:

Taxes
Who benefits from it?
Who pays for it?

And we are interested in discrimination:

Making sure that everyone gets treated equally
Is everyone equally able to get help?
Is support provided to match what people want whatever their 'race', age, gender, impairment, sexual orientation etc?

We are asking people:
- What do you want for your life?
- What do you want for the future?